BLACK BELT®

100
THE FIRST ONE HUNDRED ISSUES

By the Editors of *Black Belt*

Compiled by Robert W. Young

Edited by Sarah Dzida, Raymond Horwitz, Jon Sattler and Jeannine Santiago

Cover and Interior Design by John Bodine

All Rights Reserved
Printed in the United States of America
ISBN-10: 0-89750-173-X
ISBN-13: 978-0-89750-173-6
Library of Congress Control Number: 2008937067

First Printing 2008

Printed in Korea

(Note: Back issues are not available for purchase. Frame-suitable 9-in.-by-12-in. full-color reproductions of each cover available for purchase at www.blackbeltmag.com/covers.)

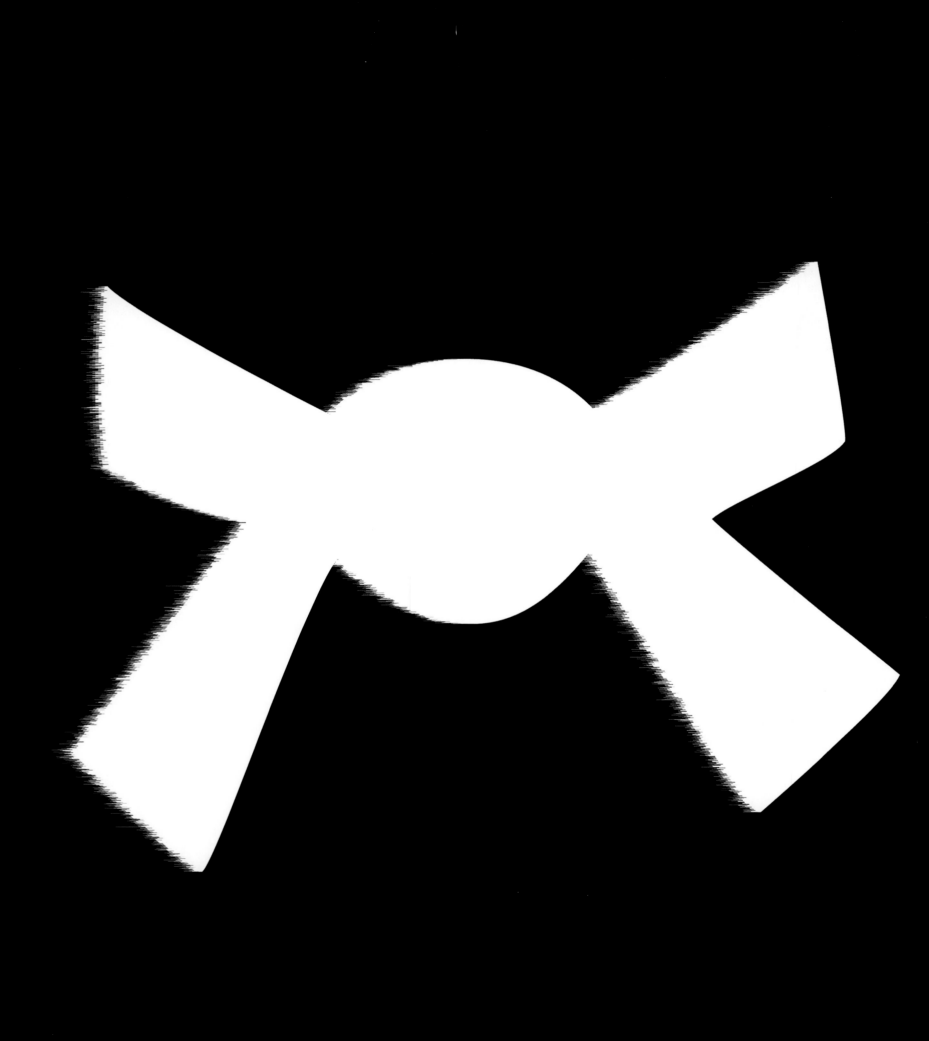

ACKNOWLEDGEMENTS

We
would
like
to
thank
all
our
readers,
both
past
and
present.

—The Editors of
BLACK BELT®

Black Belt—the original editors chose the name for this groundbreaking magazine because of its deep significance to all martial artists. When *Black Belt* first hit the stands in 1961, as the first and only resource on the martial arts, the original editors had many hopes for it. They intended that the magazine would serve as a regular resource to the martial arts community, become a forum for martial artists to communicate their enthusiasm for and knowledge of their combat style to each other, dispel the brutish and narrow martial arts stereotypes that filled the media, and remain an authentic authority by cultivating close relationships with numerous experts in the industry. Obviously, *Black Belt*'s longevity can attest to the success of these intentions, and the first 100 issues especially demonstrate how quickly readers responded to the articles, people and issues discussed in the magazine. As the current editors, we're proud to be a part of such a long tradition of excellence. We thank all our readers for their enthusiasm and loyalty, and we hope they enjoy this collection of covers and highlights from our great magazine's early years.

The Editors of *Black Belt*
2008

BLACK BELT®

100

THE FIRST ONE HUNDRED ISSUES

COVERS and HIGHLIGHTS
1961–1972

50c

Black Belt

THE MAGAZINE OF SELF-DEFENSE

VOL. I, NO. 1

● JUDO ● KARATE ● AIKIDO ● KENDO

SPECIAL JUDO ISSUE
Complete National AAU Finals

ISSUE ONE | JUNE 1961

The first issue of *Black Belt* was dated June 1961 and was 66 pages and 5-1/2 by 8-1/4 inches. The publication schedule was somewhat irregular in those early days, so don't think something is amiss when you notice that the second issue was dated January 1962, the third was April 1962 and so on.

Vol. 1, No. 1, 50 cents

▶ Jigoro Kano, founder of *kodokan* judo, is profiled; as is Lucille Hagio, a UCLA sophomore who taught a judo class for girls.

▶ America receives its introduction to *kenpo* karate through an article titled "Ed Parker, the Black-Belted Mormon."

▶ The National AAU Judo Championships take place in Fresno, California. The winners are Sumikichi Nozaki (140 pounds), Toshiyuki Seino (160 pounds), Ben Campbell (180 pounds) and George Harris (heavyweight).

▶ American President Lines offers first-class cruises from California to Japan for $510.

▶ The *aikido* adventures of Koichi Tohei, a student of founder Morihei Uyeshiba, are retold.

▶ Torao Mori, America's highest-ranked *kendo* practitioner, describes his martial education in Japan and his efforts to spread the sword art in the United States.

▶ *Black Belt* founder and former editor M. Uyehara teaches a basic aikido throw.

▶ A subscription to *Black Belt* is advertised for $3 a year.

AUTHENTIC JUDO AND KARATE INSTRUCTIONS!

BLACK BELT

K

35¢

JANUARY, 1962

The Magazine of Self-Defense

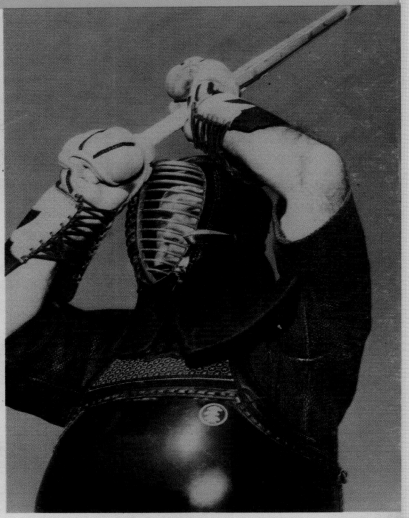

Practical Self-Defense for Women

MacDonald Carey Learns Karate

Judo at the Air Force Academy

Learn a Champion's Technique

ISSUE TWO | JANUARY 1962

The second issue of *Black Belt* wore a cover date of January 1962. It was a full-size magazine, measuring 8-1/2 by 11 inches, and included 65 black-and-white pages and a full-color cover.

Vol. 1, No. 2, 35 cents

► Life at the Kodokan, Tokyo's renowned judo headquarters, is described: After submitting an application and paying a registration fee of 85 cents, novices can train for $1.15 a month, and advanced practitioners can work out for $5.60 a month.

► Third-degree black-belt Edmund Parker becomes *Black Belt's* consultant on *kenpo* karate.

► Hidetaka Nishiyama, director and head instructor of the Japan Karate Association, arrives in Los Angeles for a six-month engagement, during which he plans to teach members of the Southern California Karate Association.

► "Mr. Judo," a story about the indomitable Gene LeBell, introduces America to a future martial arts legend.

► An associate editor profiles handicapped *kendo* practitioner Gordon Warner in "The One-Legged Swordsman."

► A visit to the Hawaii Aiki Kwai organization by *aikido* founder Morihei Uyeshiba and Nobuyoshi Tamara is chronicled.

► The swords and armor of Europe and Japan are compared in an article by the same one-legged warrior.

► Phil Porter, the man who would serve as president of the National Judo Institute and head coach of the U.S. judo team from 1980 to 1995, pens a story titled "Judo at the Air Force Academy."

► A tiny advertisement claims that Americans can live or vacation in Mexico for $150 a month, hire a maid for $12 a month, buy liquor for 80 cents a fifth (of a gallon) and eat filet mignon for 50 cents a pound.

► A special charter-subscription rate for 10 issues of *Black Belt* is offered for $3.

AUTHENTIC JUDO AND KARATE INSTRUCTIONS!

BLACK BELT K

The Magazine of Self-Defense

APRIL, 1962

35¢

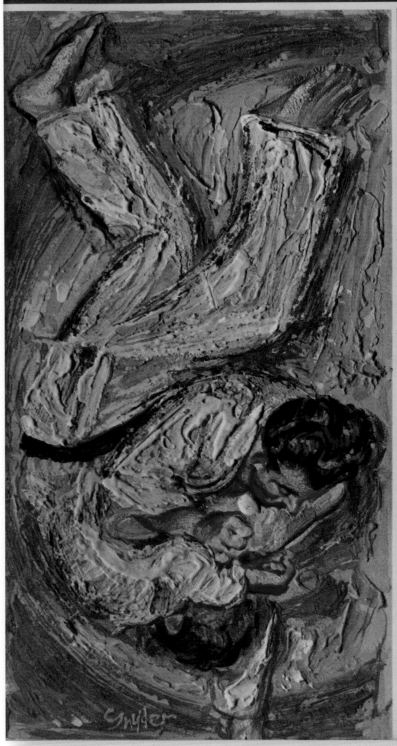

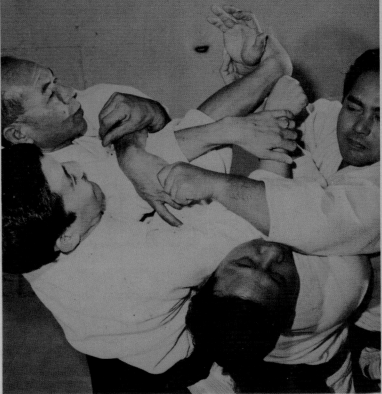

JAPANESE STUNNED BY LOSS IN WORLD JUDO TOURNEY TO DUTCHMAN

Judo in SAC Air Force

Practical Self-Defense for Women

Nick Adams with the Samurai Yen

KARATE AND AIKIDO TECHNIQUES

I S S U E   T H R E E | **A P R I L   1 9 6 2**

The third issue of *Black Belt* had a cover date of April 1962. It was a full-size magazine, measuring 8-1/2 by 11 inches, and included 66 black-and-white pages and a full-color cover.

Vol. 1, No. 3, 35 cents

▶ *What Is Karate?,* a landmark text by *kyokushin* karate founder Masutatsu Oyama, is advertised for the bargain price of $6.50.

▶ In "An Unwanted Kiss," *Black Belt's* female readers are shown how to "thwart the advances of an over-amorous assailant or even ... a 'gentleman.' "

▶ Fresh off a six-month instructional tour of Southern California, Hidetaka Nishiyama, who learned *shotokan* karate directly under Gichin Funakoshi, is profiled.

▶ The sword moves actor Toshiro Mifune used to defeat eight attackers in a film titled *Tsubaki Sanjuro* are analyzed and taught.

▶ President John F. Kennedy is shown watching members of a U.S. Army Rangers unit demonstrate their combat judo skills.

▶ Dr. William C.C. Hu sets the record straight regarding the "Historical Roots of Karate" because, as he wrote, "Sensational hunting publications mislead the public about the true origin and intent of this martial art."

▶ Dutch judo legend Anton Geesink defeats Japan's Koji Sone, winning the 1961 World Judo Championship in Paris. Stunned Japanese officials respond: Sone lost because of Geesink's "superior physical strength," the loss will be a "good opportunity for Japanese judo to reflect," and "We do not have to be pessimistic over the 1964 Olympic Games. We must, of course, watch more carefully the progress of foreign *judoka*. But isn't Geesink the only really strong foreigner now?"

▶ Back issues of *Black Belt* are offered for 50 cents each, shipping and handling included.

AUTHENTIC JUDO AND KARATE INSTRUCTIONS!

BLACK BELT

35¢

SEPTEMBER, 1962

The Magazine of Self-Defense

SELF-DEFENSE FOR WOMEN

CHURCH GETS BOOST FROM JUDO

THE HISTORY OF JUDO

KARATE AND AIKIDO

Self-Defense for Women

COLLEGE JUDO

ISSUE FOUR | SEPTEMBER 1962

The fourth issue of *Black Belt* was dated September 1962. It featured a painting of Morihei Uyeshiba, along with two photos of Master Ku Yu-Cheung pulverizing a pile of bricks, on the cover.

Vol. 1, No. 4, 35 cents

▶ The editorial addresses the problems created by sham instructors who open schools and teach poor martial arts techniques for immediate financial gain. As the French say: *Plus ça change, plus c'est la même chose.*

▶ In a letter to the editor, Dr. Richard D. Mosier of the University of California, Berkeley, makes two important observations: "There can be little doubt that … karate or kung fu existed in a highly developed form before the introduction of Buddhism into China about A.D. 520; and in this respect there can be no question but that the discipline that finally evolved as karate is of Chinese origin."

▶ The early exploits of *aikido* founder Morihei Uyeshiba are described, and rare photos of the master in his Tokyo *dojo* (training hall) are shown.

▶ A tutorial on the Japanese sword traces the development of the popular weapon from the third century to the present.

▶ Karate legend Hidetaka Nishiyama begins penning a series on the basic techniques and terminology of the self-defense art.

▶ "The Fair Sex Enjoys Judo, Too" contains a number of photos that must have been viewed as rather risqué at the time: women rolling around on the mat in extremely close contact with the opposite sex.

▶ Dr. William C.C. Hu gives a scholarly discourse on the history of judo, complete with the *kanji* (Japanese characters derived from the Chinese written language) equivalents of all the important names and terms.

▶ Ed Parker's book *Kenpo* is offered for the bargain-basement price of $6.25.

AUTHENTIC JUDO AND KARATE INSTRUCTIONS!

BLACK BELT

50¢

FEBRUARY 1963

The Magazine of Self-Defense

COLLEGE JUDO

KARATE AND AIKIDO

ISSUE FIVE | FEBRUARY 1963

The fifth issue of *Black Belt* was dated February 1963. The cover featured a painting of two battling *kendo* practitioners, a photo of a *karateka* using a knifehand strike to chop the top off an Asahi beer bottle, and a second photo of a karateka using his elbow to smash a stack of 15 roof tiles.

Vol. 1, No. 5, 50 cents

► A reader questions the authenticity of the images that appeared on the cover of the September 1962 issue. "You had photos of a karateka breaking 12 bricks with a slap of the hand," Doug Bartram writes. "Let me assure you that this feat is impossible with standard American building bricks regardless of mental concentration and physical force."

► P.M. Suski pens a very informative article about Japanese sword making, and for the benefit of the literati, he even includes the *kanji* symbols for all the Japanese terms and names.

► A short feature tells the story of Bolsa Grande High School in Garden Grove, California—the first American school to adopt kendo as part of its physical-education program.

► Judo champ Kazuo Shinohara offers advice to aspiring grapplers: "In sumo, one must master the art of pushing. In baseball, it's swinging. Originally in judo, [it was] pulling. However, I believe that a *judoist* must be able to push as well as pull; this to be done instantaneously while maintaining a strong balance."

► Thomas A. Makiyama writes: *"Black Belt,* I believe, was created to fill in the gaps in the usually distorted versions of the arts. It is therefore imperative that you attempt to give a fair picture of the arts and not be satisfied with the surface aspects as may be pointed out by a single source. While it is true that certain arts may find [more] popularity with the public, the existence of the different schools should be pointed out in the interest of fair play. If your consultants have learned about *aikido* and karate in the U.S. and not in Japan, their versions would be extremely limited. It may be that some of them have made short visits to Japan for studies, but subjects such as these cannot be learned merely by visiting Japan on a tour." [Editor's note: Letters such as these indicate that American martial artists were becoming more sophisticated and knowledgeable—and had started critically analyzing every word and every photo.]

► A sign of things to come in the form of an advertisement: *"Judo Movie,* an instructional movie, slow motion, four throws. Mugger, knifer, clubber and puncher. 8mm 180 feet. $10."

AUTHENTIC JUDO AND KARATE INSTRUCTIONS!

BLACK BELT

50¢

SUMMER, 1963

The Magazine of Self-Defense

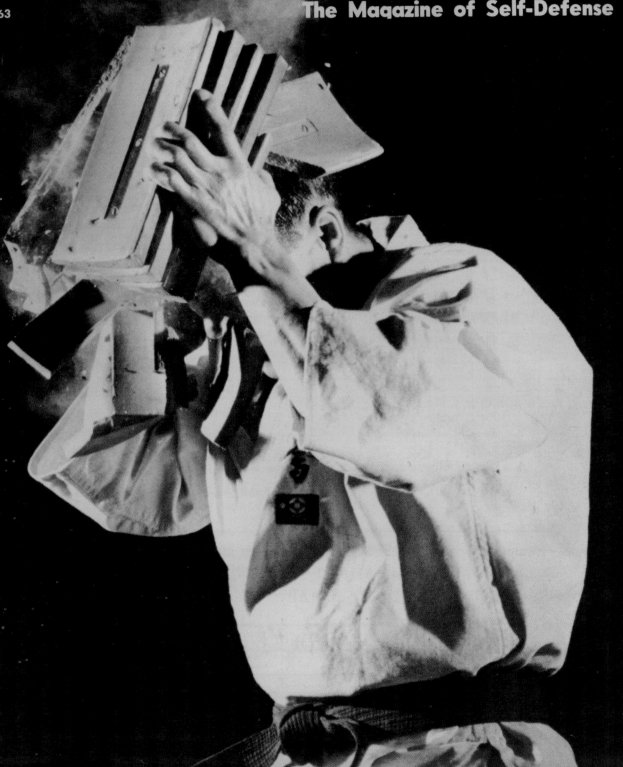

ISSUE SIX | SUMMER 1963

The sixth issue of *Black Belt* had a cover date of Summer 1963 and was 64 pages long. The cover featured a black-and-white photo of a karate master breaking five tiles on his head.

Vol. 1, No. 6, 50 cents

▶ An advertisement proclaiming "I'll make you a master of kung fu" touts a book about Chinese leg maneuvers. For some reason, the ad promises that the text will be mailed in a plain brown wrapper.

▶ In "Gama, the Lion: Master of the Arts," the life of the great Indo-Pakistani wrestler, whose proper name was Mian Ghulam Mohammed (1880 to 1960), is retold.

▶ Bargain-basement judo gear is advertised: a heavyweight double-weave uniform for $18.25, separate uniform pants for $3.50 and an imported *tatami* mat for $24 each.

▶ William S. Morris profiles a legend in "Henry S. Okazaki, Founder of American *Jujutsu*."

▶ *Judoka*-turned-*karateka* Hirakazu Kanazawa reveals his views on switching arts, training to win tournaments and using karate to become a more productive member of society.

▶ A quaint story by W.M. Hawley describes how ancient Japanese sword makers tested their blades on human targets—living and dead.

▶ "There should be one karate. People don't know where to turn to study good karate. Many good men teach wrong karate because that is all they know. Some bad men teach bad karate to take advantage of the public and to make money. Just as judo has the Kodokan, so should karate have a central organization that will set a high standard and make everyone meet it." So says *kyokushin* karate founder Masutatsu Oyama in an exclusive *Black Belt* interview.

▶ The floodgates are open: The previous issue of *Black Belt* features an ad for a judo movie, and this issue includes that same ad, along with one for an 8mm film of karate self-defense techniques. Two 50-foot reels cost $5.99 postpaid.

AUTHENTIC JUDO AND KARATE INSTRUCTIONS!

BLACK BELT

50¢

JANUARY, 1964

The Magazine of Self-Defense

COMPLETE COVERAGE OF THE FIRST
WORLD KARATE TOURNAMENT

GOJURYO KARATE

BLACK BELT
REPORTS ON HIGH SCHOOL JUDO

TECHNICAL QUESTIONS AND ANSWERS

ISSUE SEVEN | JANUARY 1964

The seventh issue of *Black Belt* had a cover date of January 1964 and was 68 pages long. The cover featured a black-and-white photo of *aikido* expert Koichi Tohei throwing an opponent.

Vol. 2, No. 1, 50 cents

► A reader from Nova Scotia, Canada, raises one of the most enduring questions in the martial arts world: "Is it possible for any person ... to take a home-study course in judo or karate and become good at it?" *Black Belt's* answer has been just as enduring: "There is no substitute for actual training, [but] basic techniques can be mastered with the help of information available in periodicals and training manuals."

► American *kenpo* karate founder Ed Parker provides coverage of the First World Karate Tournament, held July 28, 1963, at the University of Chicago Field House.

► A photo caption in "Girls Self-Defense Judo" reads, "If your assailant still fails to get the hint and persists, [raise your] hands and flick your fingers into his eyes. Another kick to his shin, to boot, may get the idea across. If these instructions fail to produce the desired results, enroll at a competent judo, karate or aikido school."

► In "Mas Oyama Speaks Out," the famed *kyokushin* karate founder and all-around tough guy regales readers with tales of terminating wild dogs "by giving them hand chops to the neck" and bulls "by first knocking off their horns with chops, then killing them with a blow of the fist to the heart."

► A Long Island, New York-based Korean instructor named Young Koo Lee explains that "there is almost no difference between the *chung do kwan* [style of *taekwondo*] and the main karate (that of the Japan Karate Association), although both of these differ from other schools of karate."

► In a feature about the Japan Karate Association headquarters, it is revealed that training under some of the top *karateka* in the Land of the Rising Sun costs a mere $5.58 a month.

► An obituary mourns the loss of Kiyose Nakae, author of one of the earliest and most influential martial arts texts: *Jiu Jitsu Complete*.

AIKIDO   JUDO   KARATE   KENDO

BLACK BELT

MARCH 1964 **The Magazine of Self-Defense** 50¢

CAPOEIRA-BRAZILIAN KICK

KENDO MASTERS FROM JAPAN

KENDO: JAPANESE FENCING

MIGHTY MITES OF THE AIR FORCE

ISSUE EIGHT | MARCH 1964

The eighth issue of *Black Belt* was dated March 1964. It featured a photograph of the perennial "Judo" Gene LeBell—whose face is barely visible but whose red hair is unmistakable—executing an *uchi mata* (inner-thigh reaping throw) on the cover.

Vol. 2, No. 2, 50 cents

► A judo brown belt from Mt. Vernon, New York, lightheartedly promises to thrash the editorial staff of *Black Belt* unless issues are published more frequently. It would be the first of many times that editors were threatened.

► A tiny ad promising to ready readers to break bricks in 100 days touts a packet of "free literature" for $5.

► The validity of the traditional Asian practice of toughening the hands by smashing them into stones and blocks is questioned for the first time in print.

► One of the earliest articles covering the rhythmic Brazilian art of *capoeira* appears. It is written by a native called Master Pastinha.

► Dr. Gordon Warner pens a piece on how to enjoy a samurai movie, in which he encourages Japanese filmmakers to concoct noble epics that are true to the past and beneficial to the nation's youth.

► A story titled "Tang Soo Do Flies High at March Air Force Base" introduces first-degree black-belt Carlos Norris (aka Chuck Norris), who headed the American Tang Soo Do Association's Southern California team.

► "The Eighteen Martial Arts of Japan" lists the traditional skills of the samurai: *ba jutsu* (art of horsemanship), *batto jutsu* (art of drawing the sword), *bo jutsu* (art of using the wooden staff), *fukumibari jutsu* (art of blowing needles), *ho jutsu* (art of gunnery), *jujutsu* (art of unarmed self-defense), *jutte jutsu* (art of protecting against sword attacks using a "police stick"), *kenjutsu* (art of fencing), *kusarigama jutsu* (art of using the iron chain with an attached blade), *kyujutsu* (art of archery), *mojiri jutsu* (art of entanglement), *naginata jutsu* (art of the halberd), *shinobi jutsu* (art of stealth or *ninjutsu*), *shuriken jutsu* (art of the throwing star), *so jutsu* (art of the long spear), *suiei jutsu* (art of swimming while wearing armor), *tanto jutsu* (art of the dagger) and *torite jutsu* (art of the rope).

BLACK BELT

The Magazine of Self-Defense

MAY-JUNE 1964

U.S. 50¢

DO·KARATE·JU JITSU·AIKIDO·KENDO

JUDO vs BOXING
History of Ju-Jitsu
Judo in Germany?
2nd Canadian
Karate Men

ISSUE NINE | MAY-JUNE 1964

The ninth issue of *Black Belt* was dated May-June 1964. It featured a color photo of *kendo* practitioner Hachiro Wada on the cover.

Vol. 2, No. 3, 50 cents

► A reader from Great Britain writes a letter to lament the state of the arts in his country. He says that in judo, the buying of rank and lack of organization are dragging the sport down, while karate is poised to take over as the most popular martial art in the nation.

► Another letter writer complained about the dearth of coverage of his particular martial art. *Black Belt* responded then the same way it does now: "[We] sincerely hope to be of service to all martial artists. It is our desire to publish news and facts about all arts. However, this is not possible without the cooperation of our readers. Articles … pertaining to each group should be submitted for possible publication."

► Dr. Philip J. Rasch writes a scientific treatise titled *"Karateka vs. Wrestler."* When the Ultimate Fighting Championship debuted in 1993, the same subject would resurface as "striker vs. grappler" and ignite the martial arts world.

► Continuing in the same vein, Dewey Lawes Falcone reports on the first widely publicized mixed-martial arts bout in America: "Judo" Gene LeBell vs. boxer Milo Savage. In case you didn't hear, LeBell choked his opponent unconscious in the fourth round.

► Robert A. Trias is listed as having received his 10th-degree black belt from the United States Karate Association.

► Following a chain of events that seems oddly similar to those that recently involved *taekwondo,* it is announced that the International Olympic Committee decided to drop judo from the 1968 games—even though it was included in the 1964 games.

► An unidentified expert declares, "Size in judo does make a difference. The concept that a small man has just as much chance as a big man was proved wrong in the last world tournament. But a small, proficient *judoka* can topple a big, unskilled person."

JUDO • KARATE • AIKIDO • KENDO

BLACK BELT

JULY-AUGUST 1964 · **The Magazine of Self-Defense** · 50 CENTS

VOLUME TWO, NUMBER FOUR

SUMO: BATTLE OF GIANTS

KARATE IN DALLAS, TEXAS

COLUMBIA UNIVERSITY WINS JUDO TOURNEY

ISSUE TEN | JULY-AUGUST 1964

The 10th issue of *Black Belt* was dated July-August 1964. It featured a color photo of sumo champion Tochinoumi on the cover.

Vol. 2, No. 4, 50 cents

▶ From a panic-stricken letter writer: "Is there any program in existence for controlling the teaching of judo to extremist groups likely to abuse the knowledge of the art? I have read numerous references in *Newsweek* to [various organizations] being 'judo trained.' "

▶ The great Ed Parker expresses his views on the state of the martial arts: Do you think karate will supersede boxing in popularity in the USA? "Sure it will—if karate is presented to the public properly. Favoritism in tournaments should be banned, and all tournaments should be open to all clubs. I'm attempting to set a precedent in a coming tournament in Long Beach (California). There won't be any forms *(kata)* contest. It will be strictly freestyle sparring *(kumite)*. From the outset I was entirely against the kata contest because I knew it was going to be difficult to choose the winner."

▶ Robert A. Trias, head of the United States Karate Association, is profiled. Trias would be inducted into the *Black Belt* Hall of Fame in 1979 and again after his death on July 11, 1989.

▶ When a reader expresses an interest in learning more about Chinese herbs that are used to condition the hands, *Black Belt* replies: "We cannot disclose the ingredients used to make liniments because some of them have an adverse affect on some people." That policy remains in effect.

▶ In a letter to the editor and a feature story, the various Japanese swords— *katana, chokuto, tachi, daisho, tanto* and *kozuka*—are described.

▶ *Black Belt* Hall of Fame member and karate legend Mike Stone places first in the brown-belt forms and brown-belt sparring divisions at the First Southwest Karate Championships in Dallas.

▶ First-degree black-belt Charles Sereff is part of a demo team that performed for the Denver Electrical Union.

▶ Wally Jay is honored by the city of Alameda, California, for leading the Island Judo Jujitsu Club to victory in 1963.

▶ Hidetaka Nishiyama and the Japan Karate Association release six reels of 8mm film of karate techniques for $98.

JUDO · KARATE · AIKIDO · KENDO

BLACK BELT

SEPT - OCT 1964   The Magazine of Self-Defense   50 CENTS

VOLUME TWO, NUMBER FIVE

KARATEKA FIGHTS THUGS

MR. AND MRS. BLACK BELT

TOUGH JUDO LEATHERNECKS
OF PARRIS ISLAND

ISSUE ELEVEN | SEPTEMBER-OCTOBER 1964

The 11th issue of *Black Belt* was dated September-October 1964. It featured a photo of Samoan *karateka* Tigi Mataali driving a hammerfist through four slabs of stone on the cover.

Vol. 2, No. 5, 50 cents

▶ Currently one of the most sought-after martial arts books in the world, *The Complete Kano Jiu-Jitsu* is offered for a mere $2.

▶ A one-time reader from Long Island, New York, opines: "From what I have seen of the people in this country who practice karate and judo, they are all nuts. I lump them into a mold of social oddballs." Although some modern martial artists might agree with that thought, only a fool would dismiss an entire subculture of sports and self-defense enthusiasts as misfits and weirdos.

▶ The 1964 National Karate Championship winners are announced: Mike Stone takes first in the brown-belt forms and brown-belt sparring divisions, and Pat Burleson becomes the national champion in the black-belt sparring division.

▶ The venerable Dr. William C.C. Hu begins his three-part discourse titled "The Origin of Tai Chi Chuan." He concludes, *"Tai chi chuan* was merely a new name for an older form of exercise whose origins are lost in antiquity. The researcher can only look forward to the day when more pertinent and reliable sources can be uncovered."

▶ In the Instructor's Profile department, Dave Hebler, a 26-year-old first-degree black belt in *kenpo,* is highlighted. Hebler would later become a bodyguard and training partner for Elvis Presley.

▶ In "Karateka Fights Thugs," the amazing anti-crime exploits of a 29-year-old Tak Kubota are retold. The 145-pound black belt prepared for his thug-fests in a unique way: "The southern island of Japan is largely a farm area, and it was easy for Kubota to receive permission to kill hogs for the market. [He] used his fists, entering the pens and instantly killing even the largest hogs with a single blow from either hand."

▶ *Judoka* George Yoshida and his New York Dojo, the roots of which date back to 1915, are profiled in "The Grand Old Man of Judo."

▶ Look how far we've come: A feature titled "My Fearless Lady" reports, "Karate technique is not overly strenuous for a woman, yet it stimulates her circulation and improves her general muscle tone better than the most exerting exercise. The result is the natural beauty of one's skin color." Furthermore, "It does wonders for a woman's figure. ... The high kicks do wonders for the thighs and hips, and the other movements keep the waistline slim."

The Magazine of Self-Defense

NOV. - DEC. 1964

BLACK BELT

50 CENTS

IS AIKIDO THE PRACTICAL
SELF-DEFENSE FOR WOMEN?

SAMBO: THE RUSSIAN'S JUDO

HOW BIG IS AMERICAN JUDO?

THE ORIGIN OF T'AI-CHI CHUAN

ISSUE TWELVE | NOVEMBER-DECEMBER 1964

The 12th issue of *Black Belt* was dated November-December 1964. It broke new ground by placing a woman—*aikido* stylist Mariye K. Yano—on the cover.

Vol. 2, No. 6, 50 cents

▶ A dedicated reader in the Marine Corps writes, "I think *Black Belt* is the greatest thing since *Playboy.*" Hear, hear!

▶ One entry in the Instructor's Profile department reads: "Chuck Norris, 24, is the president of the Osan, Korea, branch of the American Tang Soo Do Association. He was born in Ryan, Oklahoma, but attended North High School in Torrance, California, and El Camino College in El Camino, California. He is the full-time head instructor of Norris' Tang Soo Do in Redondo Beach, California. He is ranked second degree *(ni dan)* in karate and second class *(ni kyu)* in judo."

▶ Judo veteran Phil Porter estimates the number of judo practitioners in the United States at 200,000 in 1963. He says they work out in 700 amateur clubs, 300 armed forces clubs and 200 college clubs.

▶ In *Black Belt's* first coverage of *sambo,* the Russian art's history and many technical similarities to judo are examined. (Although sambo did not take off immediately, in the late 1990s it would become one of the hottest arts in no-holds-barred competition.)

▶ In an era dominated by the Japanese martial arts, a reader from Virginia writes, "Recently I met a Korean boy who told me that in his country they have a form of self-defense called *hapkido*. From the description he gave me, I suspect that it must be something like Japanese aikido. Would you please furnish additional information?" The editor's reply: "Hapkido is pronounced nearly like aikido, so we think that it's the same art."

(Actually, the names of hapkido and aikido are written with the same Chinese characters, but as we all know now, the arts are very different.)

▶ *Black Belt* details the life of Dr. Tsuyoshi Chitose and his art of *chito-ryu* karate.

▶ Expounding on the secrecy with which *tai chi chuan* used to be taught, Dr. William C.C. Hu writes, "The Chen clan monopolized tai chi chuan and kept it secret for 14 generations. The rules forbade the teaching of it to anyone outside the clan. No one was allowed to perform the art in public or engage in any occupation which necessitated the use of its skills." Aren't you glad times have changed?

Special: ANCIENT FIGHTING ARTS OF CHINA

BLACK BELT

AIKIDO—
THE LIVING ZEN

THE TIGER,
THE DRAGON
AND THE CRANE

THE
JADE-WELL
MOUNTAIN-MAN

SOUTHERN STATE
TRIES TO SET UP
JUDO-KARATE CZAR

KUNG-FU MASTER
WONG ARK-YUEY:
The Tiger
In the Moon Gate
(See story inside)

JANUARY 1965 — 50 CENTS

ISSUE THIRTEEN | JANUARY 1965

The 13th issue of *Black Belt* was dated January 1965. With it, the world's leading martial arts publication went monthly. The issue was 66 pages long and featured a color photo of Wong Ark-Yuey on the cover.

Vol. 3, No. 1, 50 cents

▶ The early days of the legendary kung fu master Wong Ark-Yuey (aka Ark Y. Wong) are detailed. In 1970 he would be inducted into the *Black Belt* Hall of Fame as Co-Instructor of the Year.

▶ It is *Black Belt* vs. Big Brother as the martial arts community rallies against proposed legislation in Louisiana that would "regulate the practice and teaching of the Oriental martial arts, including but not necessarily limited to judo, *jujutsu, aikedo* (sic), karate and the like … [by establishing a board to oversee] the licensing of students, instructors and schools."

▶ Continuing in this issue's Chinese slant, *tai chi chuan* master Cheng Man-ching is profiled. Who ever said *Black Belt* was a *gi* magazine?

▶ Judo authority Hayward Nishioka, Korean-karate expert S. Henry Cho and various Thai boxers (then called Siamese boxers) tour 10 cities as part of an athletic roadshow called "The Wonderful World of Sport."

▶ After demonstrations by Bruce Lee, Takayuki Kubota, Tsutomu Ohshima and Jhoon Rhee, Mike Stone takes top honors in the heavyweight sparring division of Ed Parker's First International Karate Championships in Long Beach, California.

▶ In the Instructor's Profile department, 27-year-old Ronald Duncan is listed as the head instructor of the Bushido School of Self-Defense in Brooklyn, New York. Duncan, with a background in *hakko-ryu jujutsu* and numerous other Japanese and Okinawan arts, would become known as the "father of American *ninjutsu.*"

▶ A letter writer from Charleston, South Carolina, gets his gi pants in a bunch: "In your September-October 1964 issue in an article about [Marine Corps] training at Parris Island, you used the term 'Tough Judo Leathernecks.' Judo is supposed to be the way of gentleness. Certainly this is not judo." Talk about being anal.

Exclusive! JUDO AT THE OLYMPICS

BLACK BELT

Powerful Arms
Cut Off Breath, Blood
In Katahojime
Judo Choke

COMPLETE
OLYMPIC JUDO
FROM TOKYO —
WITH PROFILES
OF ALL PLAYERS

OUTLAWED
JUDO CHOKE
OK'D BY JBBF

CLASSICAL
GUITARIST IS
KARATE EXPERT

INTERNATIONAL
DIRECTORY OF JUDO,
KARATE AND AIKIDO
SCHOOLS & CLUBS

FEBRUARY 1965 — 50¢

ISSUE FOURTEEN | FEBRUARY 1965

The 14th issue of *Black Belt* was dated February 1965. It was 66 pages long and featured a color photo of judo black-belt Bill Nauta being choked on the cover.

Vol. 3, No. 2, 50 cents

▶ Judo debuts as an Olympic sport. Japan strikes gold in three out of four weight classes; only Holland's Anton Geesink (open weight class) is able to break their winning streak.

▶ A reader wonders whether his solo training sessions will enable him to defend himself on the street because he "read that in the beginning, sparring did not exist and yet students of karate could hold off mobs of men due to their practice of techniques and forms." *Black Belt* replies: "We wouldn't want to tell you that you could defend yourself and then have you find out, at your expense, that we were wrong. And consider this: By constantly resisting the temptation to test yourself by starting a fight, you experience the character training that is as much a part of karate as the forms."

▶ Ken Funakoshi places first in the *kumite* (free fighting) and *kata* (forms) division at the Second All-Hawaii Karate Championship.

▶ One month after winning the International Karate Grand Championship in Long Beach, California, Mike Stone takes top honors in the sparring division at the 2nd Annual World Karate Tournament in Chicago.

▶ In the Instructor's Profile department, a 28-year-old named Kyung Ho Min (aka Ken Min) is listed as holding a fourth-degree black belt in judo and a second-degree black belt in Korean karate. In the years leading up to 1974, Min would play a pivotal role in getting *taekwondo* into the Amateur Athletic Union.

▶ "Believe me when I say this, but Japan does not have a publication near equal to *Black Belt*. When I brought the latest issue to our *dojo*, all my Japanese friends were amazed to see such a magazine." So writes a U.S. airman stationed in Tokyo.

▶ In a much-anticipated match at the United States Karate Olympics (unrelated to the Olympic Games), instructors Don Nagle and Peter Urban engage in five minutes of bare-knuckle sparring. *Black Belt's* reporter gives the edge to Nagle.

▶ A Los Angeles librarian laments the fact that every time he manages to convince his superiors to purchase a book about an obscure art known as karate, some patron steals it.

▶ A one-year subscription to *Black Belt* (12 issues) sells for a cool $5.

World's Largest Magazine of Self-Defense

BLACK BELT

Okinawa-te,
forerunner of Modern Karate

**The School That
Teaches Strangulation**

**The Legendary
Heaven and Earth Society**

MARCH 1965 - 50 CENTS

Issue Fifteen | March 1965

The 15th issue of *Black Belt* was dated March 1965. It was 66 pages long and featured a black-and-white photo of Gordon Doversola executing a flying side kick on the cover.

Vol. 3, No. 3, 50 cents

▶ In "The Legendary Heaven and Earth Society," Dr. William C.C. Hu and Fred Bleicher attempt to separate fact from fiction regarding the often-distorted history of Shaolin Temple and the Chinese martial arts.

▶ Earl Kauka, a 14-year-old student of future *Black Belt* Hall of Fame member Wally Jay, wins the lightweight judo division at the 1964 Junior Olympic AAU Age Group Championships.

▶ The tough-as-nails students of Ken Freeman's Newark, New Jersey, judo school are profiled. The secret of their success is one that would finally catch on in the mid-1990s when some boys from Brazil took over the world: strangulation techniques.

▶ In a lamentation about the then-popular disdain for protective pads, a reader exhibits the same alarmism that is now being leveled at no-holds-barred fighting: "The sadists don't seem to realize that they are doing great damage to karate in the public's eye. Parents aren't going to let their sons and daughters engage in an art that is going to cost them broken noses, split lips, broken teeth and the like."

▶ Masami Tsuruoka, a follower of *chito-ryu* karate's Tsuyoshi Chitose, earns himself a noteworthy nickname: the "father of Canadian karate."

▶ Jhoon Rhee, 32 years old and wearing a sixth-degree black belt in *taekwondo,* is featured in the Instructor's Profile department.

▶ An awe-struck reader from Atlanta writes, "I have been a reader of your magazine right from volume one, number one, and I have always been grateful enough just to have a magazine of the martial arts to overlook the clumsiness you displayed occasionally in the past. When I passed a newsstand and saw *Black Belt,* I'd say, 'There's our magazine; I hope there's just enough of us to keep it alive.' Recently, however, the magazine has been showing a grace and professionalism that seem to indicate *Black Belt* has come of age." Amen, brother.

▶ For $5.95 readers can purchase a three-volume Japanese language course to facilitate communication in the *dojo.* It is composed not of cassettes or even 8-track tapes but of 33-1/3 revolutions-per-minute records.

World's Leading Magazine Of The Martial Arts

BLACK BELT

April 1965 — 50 Cents

RUTH HORAN: JUDO INSTRUCTOR
TO 300 GIRLS A WEEK

ZEN—MOST
POWERFUL ELEMENT
OF SELF-DEFENSE

Aikido Expert
Holds Off a Half-
Dozen Attackers
At a Time

ISSUE SIXTEEN | APRIL 1965

The 16th issue of *Black Belt* was dated April 1965. It was 66 pages long and featured a color photo of fourth-degree *aikido* black-belt Tokuji Hirata fending off five attackers on the cover.

Vol. 3, No. 4, 50 cents

▶ A reader writes in to ask who the head judge with the catlike grace and the black uniform at the 1964 Karate Olympics in New York was. *Black Belt* responds: "The man in the black silk *gi* was Maung Gyi of Burma, an expert in Burmese *bando*-style karate." In later years, Gyi would become the best-known bando authority in the world.

▶ Mike Stone's 1964 triumphs at various national and international karate tournaments are discussed in a feature about the 23-year-old fighting phenom. Stone was inducted into the *Black Belt* Hall of Fame in 1971 as Competitor of the Year and in 1994 as Instructor of the Year.

▶ *Black Belt* historian Dr. William C.C. Hu digs for facts about the famed Buddhist temple in "Searching for the Shaolin Monastery." Shaolin's true role in the propagation of the Chinese martial arts remains controversial to this day.

▶ Thomas Anguay, a former pro boxer and black belt in karate, judo and *jujutsu*, gives what is believed to be the first karate demonstration in Austria.

▶ A 47-year-old Wally Jay and a 23-year-old Tim Tackett are featured in the Instructor's Profile department. Jay, of course, would go on to found small-circle jujutsu and become one of the most active seminar instructors in the world. Tackett would later migrate away from the traditional Chinese arts and establish himself as a respected *jeet kune do* teacher and author.

▶ Ruth Horan is selected for a four-page feature because she is one of a rare breed—an American woman who has attained the rank of first-degree black belt in judo. The article reports that she teaches the grappling art to 300 girls in New York City, making her a successful instructor by anyone's standards.

▶ Predating America's new-age love affair with meditation, "The Zen 'Unconscious': Highest Attainment of the Martial Arts" describes the benefits of sitting in that oh-so-comfortable lotus position.

▶ Black-and-white 8-by-10 photos of judo founder Jigoro Kano are offered for sale at the bargain-basement price of $1 each. The same company sells *bokken* (wooden training swords) for $5.

World's Leading Magazine Of The Martial Arts

BLACK BELT

MAY 1965
FIFTY CENTS

Miss Burbank 1963

Beauty Queen
Linda Carpenter Flips
Her Black Belt Husband
Dave Chow
of Hollywood
With
a Judo
Throw

Kuoshu — The Karate of South China

ISSUE SEVENTEEN | MAY 1965

The 17th issue of *Black Belt* was dated May 1965. It was 66 pages long and featured a color photo of white-belt Linda Carpenter judo-flipping black-belt husband Dave Chow on the cover.

Vol. 3, No. 5, 50 cents

▶ A reader from Vermont writes in to comment on a case of martial arts swindling that involved an unscrupulous individual who signed students up for $350 contracts, then sold them to a finance company and skipped town. The unsuspecting students were stuck footing the monthly bill. The reader's advice was as useful then as it is now: Read the fine print before signing anything.

▶ A 23-year-old Tim Tackett introduces America to *kuoshu,* the martial art of Taiwan. He would later play a key role in the Jeet Kune Do Nucleus.

▶ Jack A. Rains retells a humbling story, "A female martial arts expert in Japan was attacked by five hoodlums. She fought back, and three of the men wound up in the hospital. When her judo master heard what happened, he scolded her for not using her knowledge of *do* (the way) to sense the danger potential and avoid the neighborhood altogether."

▶ Tsutomu Ohshima, then a fifth-degree *shotokan* karate black belt, is named chairman of the United States Karate Association Technique and Research Committee.

▶ A Tiger Brand extra heavy-duty, Kodokan-approved judo *gi* (uniform) is offered for $8.90. Add two bucks for extra large.

▶ The Instructor's Profile department features more than its usual number of gems: 28-year-old *hapkido* expert and author Choi Sea-oh, 21-year-old future fighting champ Tonny Tulleners, 28-year-old judo and karate black-belt Bill Ryusaki, and 44-year-old *tang soo do* authority and 1993 *Black Belt* Hall of Fame member Ki Whang Kim.

▶ A reader takes a few shots at one of *Black Belt's* writers, claiming that the Gene LeBell-Milo Savage no-holds-barred match was less important than Savage's boxing record would indicate. The author responds that the pugilist is no "has-been" and that LeBell is certainly well-respected in the judo community.

▶ The Black Belt Directory, the predecessor to the current Dojo Directory, includes the following schools: Trias International Karate and Judo Headquarters, Ed Parker's Kenpo Karate Studio and Norris Karate School. What it must have been like to walk in off the street and train with one of those legends!

World's Leading Magazine Of The Martial Arts

BLACK BELT

JUNE 1965 — FIFTY CENTS

Deadly Bukulan — Hand-to-Hand Combat
On the Beaches of the Java Sea

ISSUE EIGHTEEN | JUNE 1965

The 18th issue of *Black Belt* was dated June 1965. It was 66 pages long and featured a color photo of *silat* stylists Rudy Ter Linden and Paul de Thouars on the cover.

Vol. 3, No. 6, 50 cents

► *Black Belt* introduces the Indonesian art of silat to the Western world.

► T. Nakayama lambastes American karate: "My rather brief stay in the United States has convinced me that the state of the martial arts here is very poor indeed. Also, I have noticed that most karate schools in the United States offer something which can hardly pass for karate." Ouch.

► An article by Takashi Ozawa discusses the history of *kendo* and its recent transplantation to the United States.

► Former contributing editor Mel Appelbaum places third in the Northeastern United States Judo Championships.

► The University of Alberta (Canada) launches a for-credit judo program.

► Former publisher M. Uyehara scolds the judo community for thinking it's cool to wear an unwashed *gi* in class. Old Japanese traditions die hard, it would seem.

► Allen Steen holds his 2nd Annual Southwest Karate Championship in Dallas. Fred Wren wins the green- and blue-belt division, Ron Moffett takes top honors in the brown-belt division, and David Moon defeats Pat Burleson to win the black-belt division.

► A reader from Southern California writes to complain that the Los Angeles City Library refuses to carry *Black Belt* because of the librarian's many misconceptions about the martial arts. Although libraries no longer censor us, many prisons do. (It is perhaps more disturbing that some prisons allow inmates to read *Black Belt*.)

► The Instructor's Profile department features Richard Kim, who holds a seventh-degree black belt in karate, a seventh degree in *jujutsu* and a fourth degree in judo. In 1986 he would be named *Black Belt's* Man of the Year.

► Reader John L. Lombrado argues that mastery of karate does not necessarily require "celibacy or unreasonably strict ethics that do not allow the participant to live a well-rounded life." Thank God.

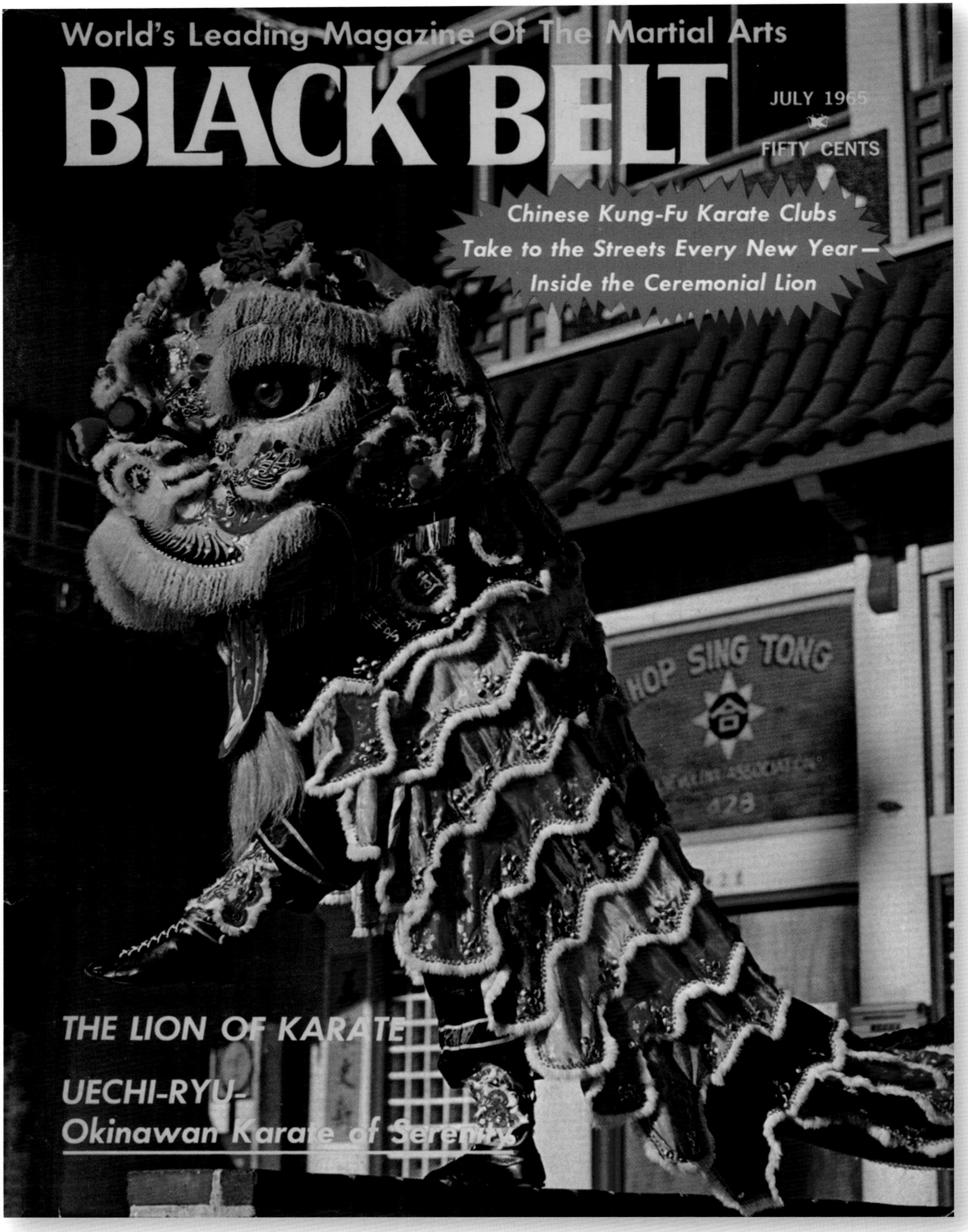

World's Leading Magazine Of The Martial Arts

BLACK BELT

JULY 1965

FIFTY CENTS

Chinese Kung-Fu Karate Clubs
Take to the Streets Every New Year—
Inside the Ceremonial Lion

HOP SING TONG

THE LION OF KARATE

UECHI-RYU—
Okinawan Karate of Serenity

Issue Nineteen | July 1965

The 19th issue of *Black Belt* was dated July 1965. It was 66 pages long and featured a color photo of a Chinese lion dancer on the cover.

Vol. 3, No. 7, 50 cents

▶ A legitimate martial arts instructor in Brooklyn, New York, offers some sage advice for prospective students seeking a *dojo:* Find out how long the establishment has been operating, inquire about accreditation with a martial arts organization, take at least one free trial lesson and ask current students if they are satisfied with the way things are run.

▶ The Instructor's Profile department features 48-year-old *aikido* inheritor Kisshomaru Uyeshiba (ninth degree) and a 27-year-old Korean master named Kim Byung-soo (fifth degree in *tae soo do,* second degree in *hapkido* and blue belt in *yudo).*

▶ When asked about the dangers of teaching karate to unsavory characters, Tetsuji Murakami, then a fifth-degree black belt, replies: "Karate is not dangerous at all. Karate is like a knife. You give a knife to a normal man, and he will put it in his pocket and use it for cutting his steak. But give that same knife to a crazy man, and he will hurt somebody. In a crazy man's hands, even a spoon is dangerous." Some 36 years later, his countrymen will be reminded of those dangers as they recover from the rampage of a kitchen-knife-wielding lunatic in an elementary school.

▶ Kanei Uechi, son of *uechi-ryu* karate founder Kanbum Uechi, tells the story of the birth of his father's art—which is claimed to be the most popular style in Okinawa.

▶ Wisdom from the pen of future *Black Belt* Hall of Fame member Henry Okazaki: "It is said of *jujutsu* that it would require 10 years of practice to win victory over oneself and 20 years to win victory over others."

▶ Long before smoking would become demonized by the American press, karate and judo cigarette lighters at $6.50 apiece are all the rage.

▶ A reader from Miami asks whether a match between a ranked *judoka* and a good *karateka* has ever taken place. *Black Belt's* answer: "We have never heard of such a match ... but sooner or later, one will probably take place." Flash-forward to 1993: The Ultimate Fighting Championship debuts in Denver, and grappling expert Royce Gracie rises to the top.

▶ The Martial Arts Supplies Company proudly announces the availability of a new 16mm movie of authentic karate, *iaido, kendo* and *naginata* demonstrations. The cost is a cool $200 for a 30-minute reel. Thank you, Panther Productions, for eventually putting an end to that madness.

JUDO: AAU National Championships

BLACK BELT

AUGUST — FIFTY CENTS

KARATEMEN
of the
**2nd Armored
Division**

**Grand Champion
Nishioka
Flips Opponent**

ISSUE TWENTY | AUGUST 1965

The 20th issue of *Black Belt* was dated August 1965. It was 66 pages long and featured a black-and-white photo of judo legend Hayward Nishioka, who had just won the AAU Grand Championship, on the cover.

Vol. 3, No. 8, 50 cents

▶ A reader from South Africa writes to ask about the legitimacy of a local self-proclaimed 10th-degree judo black belt who advertises his rank despite an official announcement from the Kodokan that no one higher than sixth degree exists outside Japan. That problem—the spontaneous generation of rank and the lack of an overseeing entity to set the record straight—continues to plague the martial arts to this day.

▶ A Milwaukee reader writes, "Although *Black Belt* has not yet achieved the journalistic sophistication that comes with years of publication experience, it is doing an admirable job of offering to the reader the positive aspects of the martial arts." Thank you very much ... We think.

▶ The president of the International Judo Federation estimates that more than 100,000 Americans practice the grappling art.

▶ Osamu Ozawa, a *Black Belt* Hall of Fame member, teaches karate's celebrated *shuto* (knife hand).

▶ Sea Oh Choi introduces America to the relatively unknown Korean art of *hapkido*. Launching an era of controversy, he states that the founder, Choi Yong-sul, was a Korean who studied *daito-ryu aikijujutsu* under Sogaku Takeda in Japan.

▶ A quality *bokken* (wooden practice sword) sells for $5, and a wooden *tanto* (knife) goes for $3.

▶ The Instructor's Profile department features Gen. Choi Hong-hi, the 47-year-old president of the Korea Taekwondo Association; and Jimmy Woo, a 50-year-old kung fu expert from Canton, China.

▶ Ed Parker's Second International Karate Championship is scheduled for the Long Beach (California) Auditorium. Only three weight classes will be used.

▶ *Black Belt* Hall of Fame member Hayward Nishioka admits to having been impressed by the advice of judo teammate and future U.S. Sen. (Colorado) Ben Campbell: "Fifty years from now when they look at the record books, the only name they see will be the name of the guy who won. It won't say he won by decision; it won't say so-and-so got out there and played good, clean, stand-up judo and finished only fourth. If you have to get him down to win, get him down—it doesn't matter how. Never mind picture-book throws. Just get out there and wipe the guy up, and don't worry about how you do it."

World's Leading Magazine Of The Martial Arts

BLACK BELT

50 CENTS

SEPTEMBER 1965

Karateka Kubota shatters
100 lb. ice block
with
Tameshi-wari
technique.

JUDO BLACK BELT WITH ONE LEG

ISSUE TWENTY-ONE | SEPTEMBER 1965

The 21ˢᵗ issue of *Black Belt* was dated September 1965. It was 66 pages long and featured a color photo of Tak Kubota breaking a 100-pound slab of ice on the cover.

Vol. 3, No. 9, 50 cents

► When asked whether he would knowingly teach karate to a person who wanted merely to become a better street fighter, Tak Kubota replies: "No. Karate is not primarily for fighting. First, it is a sport and only secondarily a method of self-defense. Everyone who enters my school signs a release. It states that if, in our judgment, they use karate to willfully harm others, I can expel them from the school."

► In response to the readers' hunger for how-to articles, Osamu Ozawa teaches karate's *seiken choku tsuki* (forefist straight counter-punch), and Hayward Nishioka gives a crash course in judo's *ippon seoinage* shoulder throw.

► Future *Black Belt* Hall of Fame member Wally Jay describes his "progressive judo" as a blend of ordinary judo, *jujutsu, aikido,* kung fu and boxing. And you thought mixing arts was a modern phenomenon!

► The Korean government and Gen. Choi Hong-hi decide to send a *taekwondo* mission to 18 nations in an effort to spread the kicking art around the world. Each stop will last for two months, during which demonstrations will take place.

► Anton Geesink, the world champion of judo, is cast as Samson in an Italian flick titled *Samson and Delilah.* A song about the martial arts world's most famous grappler is reported to be a hit in the Netherlands.

► The Instructor's Profile department features the 43-year-old Masutatsu Oyama, the founder of *kyokushin* karate. He is listed as having a black belt in karate and being proficient in judo, *daito-ryu* and *aikijutsu.*

► At the 1965 Salt Lake City Regional Karate Championships, Dan Inosanto places second in the lightweight black-belt division, while Ed Parker coaches his men to victory in the team division.

► A concerned mother from Philadelphia writes to complain about two martial arts icons: "Mike Stone and Allan Steen should be barred from all tournaments. Mike Stone is an animal. He knows nothing about the art of karate or self-control. Karate is a beautiful art, and there are many young fellows that would like to practice it, but seeing Stone perform will scare them away. Allan Steen is closely following him. They are barbarians in my eyes."

World's Leading Magazine of the Martial Arts

BLACK BELT

OCTOBER 1965   50 CENTS

Karatemen of Japan
form the
ALL JAPAN KARATE ORG.
(Zen Nihon Karate-do Rengo)

CAN U.S. KARATEMEN UNITE?

ISSUE TWENTY-TWO | OCTOBER 1965

The 22nd issue of *Black Belt* was dated October 1965. It was 66 pages long and featured a black-and-white photo of Osamu Ozawa and James Kwan on the cover.

Vol. 3, No. 10, 50 cents

▶ Gene LeBell's classic text, *The Handbook of Judo,* sells for $1.

▶ The modern history of karate is retold in a feature that describes the state of the art in Japan.

▶ In a review of Masutatsu Oyama's *This Is Karate,* Dr. Philip J. Rasch says of stone-breaking techniques: "[They] are simply a drill method, not the essence of karate. The important part of the feat, [Oyama] insists, is self-confidence."

▶ The martial arts of the French Foreign Legion are outlined in a *Black Belt* exclusive.

▶ In a survey of the martial arts in Finland, it is revealed that there are 17 black belts, 14 of whom are first degree, in the entire nation.

▶ Gunji Koizumi, the man who brought judo to the United Kingdom, dies at age 79.

▶ A reader gripes about comments *Black Belt's* previous editor made in the June 1965 issue. It seems that the former staffer said that combat is what first attracts people to the martial arts and that if a person does not approve of that, he should take up gymnastics or philosophy. "I object to the implication that combat effectiveness is the ultimate purpose of the study of the martial arts," he writes.

▶ A three-volume karate training film, shot in 8mm and totaling 45 minutes, goes for the reasonable sum of $45.

▶ The government of South Africa is up in arms over the impending visit of a band of Japanese karate experts. "What do you think would happen if 20,000 Bantus (Africans) learned karate?" local resident Sebastion Hawkins asks. "They could have this country in chaos overnight."

BLACK BELT

World's Leading Magazine of the Martial Arts

NOVEMBER 1965 🅚 **50¢**

Karate's Flying Side Kick
(Yoko-Tobi-Geri)

Shows Grace of Shotokan Style

ISSUE TWENTY-THREE | **NOVEMBER 1965**

The 23rd issue of *Black Belt* was dated November 1965. It was 66 pages long and featured a color painting of a flying side kick on the cover.

Vol. 3, No. 11, 50 cents

▶ *Aikido Self-Defense,* a text by the controversial Bruce Tegner, is ripped to shreds in a *Black Belt* book review.

▶ Martial arts icon Charles Sereff pens an article that introduces readers to the Korean art of *moo duk kwan tang soo do.*

▶ Two 50-foot reels of Ed Parker in action—which amounts to about eight minutes of screen time—sell for $5.99 postpaid.

▶ The Instructor's Profile department features 25-year-old Allen Steen, who holds a black belt from the Jhoon Rhee Karate Institute.

▶ Dr. William C.C. Hu investigates the connection between Bodhidharma and the *I Chin Ching* text.

▶ The U.S. Air Force uses judo to condition its junior officers and teach them how to defend themselves.

▶ *Black Belt* interviews Koichi Tohei: Why don't more women practice *aikido?* "Because they are afraid to fall." Why aren't there more aikido schools in the United States? "Until an instructor knows the art physically and mentally, he can't do a good job. It would be like the blind leading the blind."

▶ Mike Stone beats Tonny Tulleners to take the title at Ed Parker's 1965 International Karate Championship in Long Beach, California. Steve Sanders and Arnold Urquidez win in the white-belt division.

▶ *Kyokushin* karate founder Mas Oyama visits the Karate School of Chicago and inspects its facilities.

▶ A letter writer suggests limiting tournament participation to black belts. No doubt he would be thrilled at the National Blackbelt League's events, in which under-belts are not allowed to compete.

BLACK BELT

World's Leading Magazine of the Martial Arts

DECEMBER, 1965 50 Cents

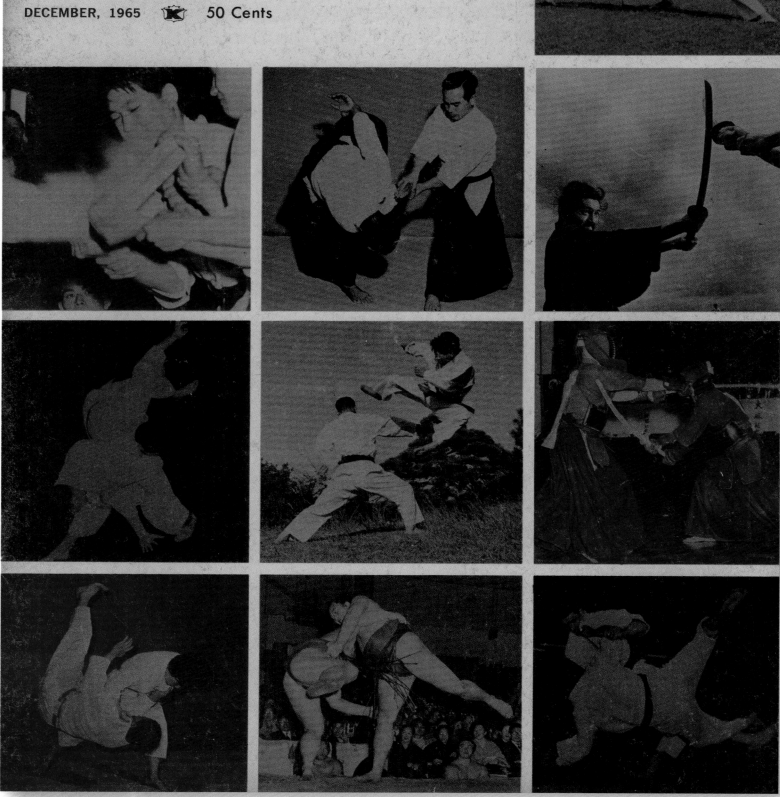

ISSUE TWENTY-FOUR | DECEMBER 1965

The 24th issue of *Black Belt* was dated December 1965. It was 66 pages long and featured a color montage of Japanese arts—including karate, judo, *kendo*, *aikido* and sumo—on the cover.

Vol. 3, No. 12, 50 cents

► A reader from Vancouver, Canada, cites a recent letter to the editor that asked whether book-based forms practice really prepares a person to defend himself. He then recounts an episode in which he, after undergoing just that type of training, was forced to fend off three thugs in a parking lot. Chalk one up for the power of the print media.

► More than 4,000 spectators show up for the second annual International Karate Tournament in Long Beach, California. Among the winners are Mike Stone, Steve Sanders, Arnold Urquidez, Skipper Mullins and Tonny Tulleners. The demonstrators include Ed Parker, Chuck Norris, Ark Y. Wong, Fumio Demura, Jhoon Rhee, Tak Kubota, Tsutomu Ohshima and Dan Inosanto.

► Future *Black Belt* Hall of Fame member Osamu Ozawa releases a three-reel set of 8mm film depicting the basic stances, blocks, strikes and kicks of karate. The price: $45.

► Two foreign-affairs features profile the judo culture in Yugoslavia and the karate explosion in South Africa.

► "Karate is not a beautiful art," a practitioner from Hawaii writes. "It is a fighting art, and fighting is never beautiful. The ancients created it to protect themselves from enemies, not to be a field-day spectator event."

► A feature article focuses on S. Henry Cho, a Korean national who teaches the *chi do kwan* (also spelled *ji do kwan*) style of *taekwondo,* which was referred to as "Korean karate" back in the days before Americans had gained much exposure to the art.

► An extra-large, heavyweight, double-weave judo *gi* sells for $18.25, while a lighter-weight karate uniform goes for $9.75.

► *Black Belt's* resident historian, Dr. William C.C. Hu, examines the issue of whether the landmark text *I Chin Ching,* often attributed to Bodhidharma, was a product of India or China.

► A group that calls itself the Buffalo Black Belt Society vows to police the ranks of the martial arts in upstate New York. Fake masters beware!

World's Leading Magazine of Self-Defense

BLACK BELT

JANUARY 1966 ✦ 50 CENTS

JUDO LIFTING HIP THROW
(tsurikomi-goshi)

A difficult but good
point getter in
competition

Issue Twenty-Five | January 1966

The 25th issue of *Black Belt* was dated January 1966. It was 66 pages long and featured a color painting of two judo players on the cover.

Vol. 4, No. 1, 50 cents

▶ When an irate reader complains about several opinions expressed in an article, *Black Belt* responds: "You must keep in mind that the statements made by an author do not reflect the magazine's philosophy. An unbiased, unprejudiced, impersonal article tends also to be uninteresting. You said each contributor should maintain the utmost respect for other points of view. We agree with you, but this does not preclude a contributor from voicing his own."

▶ *Black Belt* breaks new ground by running a photo of a partially nude woman from New Guinea. (And you thought *National Geographic* was the only one.)

▶ Japan launches a campaign to get judo back into the 1968 Olympics, and Canada pledges to support the effort if Japan will, in turn, support Canada's bid to host the next Winter Games. Politics, politics.

▶ In the continuous debate over whether Bodhidharma actually penned the *I Chin Ching* text, Dr. William C.C. Hu reveals that an 1881 addendum to a 12th-century poem was the first written reference to the Indian monk's having taught yogic exercises at Shaolin Temple.

▶ The legendary Tsutomu Ohshima, a student under *shotokan* founder Gichin Funakoshi, criticizes American tournaments: "If karate is going to degenerate into an elaborate, unrealistic sport, then we would do better to return to the original method of practicing only *kihon* (basics) and *kata* (forms) without competition."

▶ A stink is raised over a previous issue's photo depicting a martial artist wearing tennis shoes in competition. One reader even wants to pass a rule "outlawing" all types of footwear in tournaments.

▶ *Black Belt* gives rave reviews to *Judo Saga,* a 1943 martial arts film directed by Akira Kurosawa.

▶ The Instructor's Profile department features Nick Cerio, a 28-year-old brown-belt assistant instructor. Cerio, who passed away in 1998, would go on to become one of the most prominent *kenpo* instructors in the world.

▶ A reader asks what he should do now that his hand-conditioning routine has left him with a sharp pain and a middle knuckle that is three times its normal size. He reports, "It seemed like a bag of blood." Stop it immediately and get thee to a qualified instructor, he is admonished.

BLACK BELT

World's Leading Magazine of Self-Defense

FEBRUARY 1966 ☒ 50 CENTS

Geesink Retires...

Isao Inokuna — New World Champ In Action

ISSUE TWENTY-SIX | FEBRUARY 1966

The 26th issue of *Black Belt* was dated February 1966. It was 66 pages long and featured a color painting of *judoka* Isao Inokuna on the cover.

Vol. 4, No. 2, 50 cents

► A South African judo master issues an open challenge: His three sons will take on any three Japanese judoka anytime anyplace. The reason: The Kodokan refuses to admit the boys into the International Judo Federation.

► *Black Belt* devotes a record-breaking 20 pages to its coverage of the Fourth World Judo Championships in Rio de Janeiro, Brazil, and a short profile of Dutch standout Anton Geesink.

► *Nippon kenpo* is introduced to the American public. Practitioners suit up in boxing gloves, a chest protector and a baseball catcher's mask before unleashing full-contact kicking, punching and grappling techniques. Instructors advise them not to use prearranged movement sequences as taught in *kata:* "Students are encouraged to improvise and change their tactics when engaged in face-to-face contests. 'If you follow a form, your opponent might be able to guess your next move,' [instructor] Goki Kuniya says."

► Hayward Nishioka places third in the fourth-degree black-belt division of the Western States Invitational Grade Limit Judo Championships.

► *Black Belt* heartily recommends *The Crest of Man,* an ultra-realistic Japanese sword-fighting film.

► An acerbic New Yorker takes a potshot at China's premier soft art: "I recently witnessed a *tai chi* demonstration and couldn't for the life of me understand how [it] could be used to defeat an angry mosquito."

► A reader from New Mexico writes to express his opinion of martial artists creating new styles. "With much regret, I read that such an outstanding karate master as Tak Kubota has decided to start a new style, his *gosoku-ryu.* Such masters sacrifice the ideal of a unified world karate to build up their own self-esteem." Apparently, it was OK for ancient masters to create new arts but not for modern masters to do the same.

► After a number of readers express their desire to see more in-depth articles in their favorite magazine, *Black Belt* announces that it will begin running detailed technical stories that appeal to intermediate and advanced practitioners. (As a side note, our 2001 reader survey indicated that the average *Black Belt* reader has trained for eight years.)

► A size-5 heavyweight karate uniform sanctioned by the Japan Karate Association sells for $13.75.

World's Leading Magazine of Self-Defense

BLACK BELT

MARCH 1966   50 CENTS

The Cat Man of Karate —
Gogen Yamaguchi heads
Goju school

ISSUE TWENTY-SEVEN | MARCH 1966

The 27th issue of *Black Belt* was dated March 1966. It was 66 pages long and featured a color painting of Gogen "The Cat" Yamaguchi on the cover.

Vol. 4, No. 3, 50 cents

► After serving as a referee at the Canadian National Exhibition Judo Championship, Wally Jay admits to having made a mistake during a match: "I was confused and really goofed. I later wrote to [the competitor] and apologized. I had driven 3,000 miles in four and a half days to be on time to officiate for two afternoons and evenings." It's too bad more modern-day officials and competitors don't share his humility.

► At the national championships of the All America Karate Federation, which is billed as a series of United States-vs.-Japan grudge matches, Ray Dalke takes top honors and Frank Smith ties for third. In attendance are Masatoshi Nakayama (*shotokan* karate), Kenei Mabuni (*shito-ryu* karate), Hironori Ohtsuka (*wado-ryu* karate) and Gosei and Goshi Yamaguchi (*goju-ryu* karate).

► When queried about the prowess of Russian *judoka,* Hayward Nishioka says they are very strong and have been known to use *sambo* techniques to surprise their opponents.

► In Boston, the Northeastern Invitational Karate Tournament is reportedly the first major event to use chest protectors made of fiberglass.

► *Black Belt* correspondent Kim Pyung-soo covers Korea's National Athletic Meet, which attracted more than 14,000 competitors and included *yudo* (judo), *taekwondo, ssirum* wrestling, *kumdo (kendo)* and wrestling events.

► The secret behind Gogen Yamaguchi's ubiquitous nickname is revealed—well, sort of. "They call him the 'Cat,' " A. Sonny Palabrica writes. "Nobody seems to know quite how he got the name. Some say that the American GIs stationed in Japan after World War II were the first to dub him with it because he walked so softly in the *dojo* they never knew when he glided up behind them."

► In the Instructor's Profile department, Robert Cheezic, the 26-year-old head instructor of American Tang Soo Do of Connecticut, is featured. The master now oversees the Cheezic Tang Soo Do Federation and has trained more than 300 students to black-belt level.

► Roberta Jane Trias is appointed executive secretary of the United States Karate Association.

► Korea begins construction of the world's first four-year judo college.

► *Black Belt* announces its new subscription rates: 12 issues for $5.

BLACK BELT

World's Leading Magazine of Self-Defense

APRIL 1966   50 CENTS

JUDO – A Growing Spectator Sport
How You Can Enjoy A Judo Match

ISSUE TWENTY-EIGHT | APRIL 1966

The 28th issue of *Black Belt* was dated April 1966. It was 66 pages long and featured a color painting of judo referee Takahiko Ishikawa on the cover.

Vol. 4, No. 4, 50 cents

▶ "Learn karate through the magic of 8mm film," heralds an ad that offers two 50-foot reels of Ed Parker in action for $5.99 postpaid.

▶ Japanese judo champ Isao Inokuma confesses, "My father wanted me to take up judo because he thought karate was too dangerous."

▶ In a monumental event pitting Japan's best against America's finest, Kenneth Funakoshi of Hawaii defeats Hideo Ozawa, clinching a 3-2 victory for the United States.

▶ *Black Belt* introduces its readers to *sikaran,* the lost art of Philippine foot fighting. Its techniques fall into two categories: paralyzing kicks and killing kicks.

▶ "Authentic *dojo* sandals," a sort of *tatami* slipper, sell for $1.50 a pair.

▶ Ten Old World nations band together to form the Union of European Karate. Spain does not join because its leader, Gen. Francisco Franco, has banned the self-defense arts because of their "savage and brutal" nature.

▶ *Goju-ryu* karate's Gogen Yamaguchi teaches that breathing exercises can harden a man to the point at which he can absorb a kick or punch without feeling pain.

▶ Future *Black Belt* Hall of Fame member Thomas LaPuppet places first in the black-belt division at S. Henry Cho's All-American Open Karate Championships.

▶ *Aikido* founder Morihei Uyeshiba celebrates his 86th birthday in his Tokyo dojo. He says he's pleased with the progress of his art in the United States.

▶ In an early example of what has become a common critique of the martial arts industry, a reader says the continuing usage of Japanese terms to identify judo and karate moves is a handicap.

▶ A *karateka* from Winnipeg, Canada, opines: "Free-fighting competitions serve only to bring out the street fighters in droves, plunging the art of karate down to the depths of a senseless fighting sport." How fortunate it is that K-1, PRIDE and the Ultimate Fighting Championship did not exist back then.

BLACK BELT

World's Leading Magazine of Self-Defense

MAY 1966 ❈ 50 CENTS

HONBU DOJO — Testing Ground for Aikido's Future Leaders

EXTRA: Top 20 Judomen in U.S.

ISSUE TWENTY-NINE | MAY 1966

T he 29th issue of *Black Belt* was dated May 1966. It was 66 pages long and featured a color painting of Waka Uyeshiba, son of *aikido's* Morihei Uyeshiba, on the cover.

Vol. 4, No. 5, 50 cents

▶ Young men at the *aikido honbu dojo* in Tokyo must endure three years of hellish training under Morihei Uyeshiba if they want to become full-fledged instructors and rake in a cool $15 a month.

▶ Holland's Willem Ruska is touted as the successor to retired judo legend Anton Geesink.

▶ Back issues of *Black Belt* sell for 60 cents a copy if you're a subscriber, $1 a copy if you're not.

▶ The editor laments the current state of the martial arts: "It is not too far-fetched to suggest that the karate movement in this country could founder because of a lack of trust in the art and its followers." If he could have looked ahead to 2002, he would have been comforted to see that the arts are still going strong.

▶ *Black Belt* names the top-20 judo men in the United States. No.1 through No. 5 are Richard Walters, Gisuke Tomoda, James Bregman, Hayward Nishioka and Makoto Ohbayashi.

▶ Kei Tsumura explains the art behind Japan's haiku poetry. Our favorite: "Life and battle end, To the mighty ovation, Of one hand clapping."

▶ An Atlanta-based psychotherapist analyzes the martial arts and concludes that after training in aikido, judo and karate, he observed personal growth in his ability to appropriately express physical aggression, to avoid being vengeful and to become a student again.

▶ The Instructor's Profile department features 24-year-old Louis Casamassa of Bethlehem, Pennsylvania. A student of judo, aikido and karate, he would go on to helm Red Dragon Karate, which now operates in California and Utah as well as Pennsylvania.

▶ When a reader writes to ask whether there is a national karate championship held in Japan, *Black Belt* responds: "The four major Japanese karate organizations are trying to organize such an annual tournament. ... There is no such thing as a national champion of the U.S. [because] the American karate organizations have never been able to get together to hold a true national championship." Despite the claims of hundreds of current national and world champions, that statement still holds true.

BLACK BELT

World's Leading Magazine of Self-Defense

JUNE 1966 50 CENTS

The 1966 Sumo Season Gets Underway

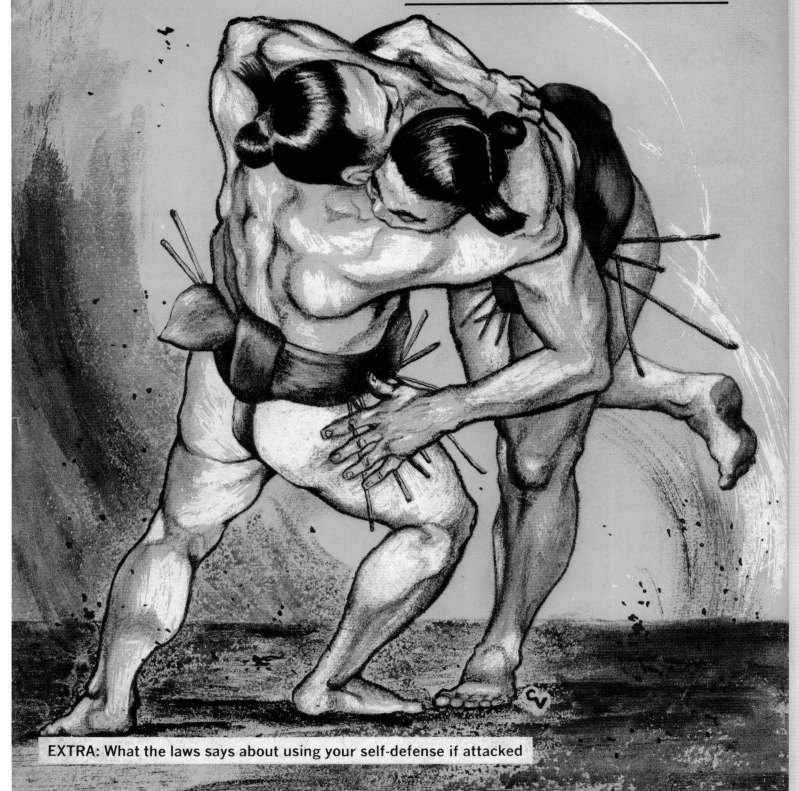

EXTRA: What the laws says about using your self-defense if attacked

Issue Thirty | June 1966

The 30th issue of *Black Belt* was dated June 1966. It was 66 pages long and featured a color painting of two sumo wrestlers on the cover.

Vol. 4, No. 6, 50 cents

▶ Renowned martial arts author Robert W. Smith takes *Black Belt* writer Dr. William C.C. Hu to task over Hu's criticisms of Smith's statements about Bodhidharma and the Chinese martial arts.

▶ In a story describing the rise of the fighting arts in the Philippines, Emanuel Querubin writes, "Another native art that closely follows the rudiments of *arnis* is *silat*. Silat makes use of sabers and daggers instead of rattan and wooden canes. It flourished as a secret form of combat exclusive to the royal families of the southernmost and predominantly Moslem section of the country."

▶ Korea correspondent Kim Pyung-soo co-writes an article about *ssirum* wrestling, which is his nation's version of sumo: "The top Korean heavyweights usually weigh more than 200 pounds, which is heavy for a Korean. But they are almost pygmylike in comparison to beefy professional Japanese sumo wrestlers, who sometimes get up to 400 pounds."

▶ Kay Tsuruoka of Toronto becomes Canada's first female black belt under the All-Japan Karate-do Association.

▶ The Japan Judo Federation considers new regulations that will discourage "runaway tactics" and encourage more aggressive tournament play.

▶ Two Chicago karate instructors are found not guilty of charges that they attempted to dynamite a competitor's *dojo*.

▶ Gunzi Koizumi, founder of British Judo, commits suicide at age 80. His chosen method for his self-induced demise: the gas stove.

▶ Vice President Hubert Humphrey is reportedly impressed by a martial arts demonstration performed by Korean troops stationed in Vietnam.

▶ The Portuguese colony of Macao, situated 40 miles west of Hong Kong, hosts a team of Thai boxers and a delegation of 29 Japanese sumo behemoths.

▶ The Korean art of *hapkido* celebrates its one-year anniversary in Germany.

▶ A reader questions the statements made by the self-proclaimed martial arts masters who advertise in various men's magazines.

BLACK BELT

World's Leading Magazine of Self-Defense

JULY 1966 • 50 CENTS

The
SAMURAI'S
Code
of
Bushido

ISSUE THIRTY-ONE | JULY 1966

T he 31st issue of *Black Belt* was dated July 1966. It was 66 pages long and featured a color painting of Toshiro Mifune on the cover.

Vol. 4, No. 7, 50 cents

▶ In an age of innocence, a New York-based martial artist writes: "I have just met a yellow belt in *aikido* who demonstrated the unbendable-arm trick. As a *judoka,* I am wondering why *ki* has not been used in contests. A judoka with an aikido or *tai chi* background would be able to resist any attempt at being thrown and could turn the attack into a fast *ippon* (point)."

▶ An 8mm movie of the International Karate Championships, at which Mike Stone defends his title, costs $11.98.

▶ Kam Yuen, the man who would become David Carradine's instructor during the filming of *Kung Fu,* objects to statements a writer made about the relationship between Okinawan karate and kung fu: "To believe that techniques in modern karate are surpassing the techniques of its ancestor [kung fu] is wishful thinking."

▶ Kisshomaru Uyeshiba, son of aikido-founder Morihei Uyeshiba, tours the East Coast of the United States.

▶ A multipart article titled "The Monks Were Afraid of Bandits and Wild Beasts" enlightens the West about the history of the Korean arts.

▶ A new unification plan is hatched by Ed Parker, Jhoon Rhee, S. Henry Cho, Tsutomu Ohshima, Tak Kubota, Fumio Demura and U.S. Sen. Milton Young (North Dakota). It will attempt to form a national karate organization designed to do away with the infighting that permeates the American martial arts scene.

▶ An alarmist piece warns of the impending demise of traditional wrestling in Japan: "Sumo is beginning to show telltale signs of age. It's a little creaky, even more old-fashioned and losing admirers to younger and more glamorous rivals. It is also suffering from the most fatal of ailments: amnesia at the box office." Not to worry. The combative sport is still going strong in 2002 and in Japan is second in popularity only to baseball.

▶ Dr. William C.C. Hu dissects *bushido,* the fighting code of the samurai.

▶ A group of Japanese students tour the United States to demo a then-unknown art: *taijutsu.* It's billed as a combination of *jujutsu, kendo* and karate.

▶ The Chicago Police Department begins teaching judo to the city's meter maids. "The idea is to give the young women training to protect themselves from molesters and thieves who might want to rob them of their collection money," the reporter explains.

SPECIAL: CONTROVERSY ENGULFS 1966 AAU JUDO CHAMPIONSHIPS

BLACK BELT

AUGUST 1966 ☀ 50 CENTS

Is Anton Geesink
Planning to Come
Out of Retirement?

ISSUE THIRTY-TWO | AUGUST 1966

The 32nd issue of *Black Belt* was dated August 1966. It was 66 pages long and featured a color painting of *judoka* Anton Geesink on the cover.

Vol. 4, No. 8, 50 cents

► In a three-page ad for martial arts books, a whopping 45 percent of the titles are dedicated to judo.

► In a letter to the editor, karate legend Richard Kim writes: "Karate is supposed to instill the qualities of virtue, integrity and wisdom, but it appears that ambition, cupidity and duplicity have taken hold on the American scene."

► *Black Belt* reports that recently retired Dutch judo sensation Anton Geesink may be planning a comeback.

► When a martial arts neophyte asks whether karate practitioners have to register their hands as lethal weapons, *Black Belt* answers: "At one time in Japan, a *karateka* was required to register his hands and so was this true in Hawaii. But the growth of karate in both places compelled the police to stop this practice."

► In an effort to unite its martial arts community, the German Judo Federation tries to assimilate the nation's karate clubs.

► Hawaii's prison guards learn karate and judo to better handle uppity convicts.

► A four-page feature titled "A Communist Swinger" profiles Yugoslav judo man Radovan Krajnovic.

► The First Japanese National Sambo Championship takes place in Kyoto.

► Japanese sumo star Wakahaguro is arrested in Tokyo after reportedly smuggling three handguns and 49 rounds of ammo into his country and selling one weapon to a gangster. He gets 18 months in the big house—and we do mean *big*.

► *Moo duk kwan tang soo do* expert Richard Chun is featured in the Instructor's Profile department.

► When a disgruntled instructor from Cleveland has the applications he and his staff sent for inclusion in said department returned to him, he writes: "We have decided to start by ourselves a magazine which would cover much more of the martial arts and stick closer to the American way. Most of my 200 students do not wish to purchase your magazine since it covers too much Oriental history, religions and attitudes." *Black Belt* responds, "All we did was ask for verification that your instructors' ranks are what they claim to be."

BLACK BELT

World's Leading Magazine of Self-Defense.

SEPTEMBER 1966 50 CENTS

Mas Oyama —
Karate is for
the Rugged

ISSUE THIRTY-THREE | SEPTEMBER 1966

The 33rd issue of *Black Belt* was dated September 1966. It was 66 pages long and featured a color painting of Mas Oyama on the cover.

Vol. 4, No. 9, 50 cents

► The United States Judo Federation plans to expand its youth training program exponentially, eventually encompassing every high school in the nation.

► In part two of his history of the Korean martial arts, Kim Pyung-soo writes: "During the Japanese occupation of Korea, only two faint sparks remained as a reminder of the past glories of [the art that was called] *kwon bup.* They were *tae kyon* and *pak chi gi.* Tae kyon was a form of foot fighting, and pak chi gi was a form of butting with the forehead, which can be very effective and very painful for the opponent—a fact learned the hard way by Russian soldiers who occupied the country briefly after World War II."

► In a letter to the editor, a reader asks, "Why in karate don't they make use of slipping the head to the right or left in evading punches, leaving both hands free for counters?" Answers, anyone?

► Former U.S. judo champ Ben Campbell holds what may be the first martial arts training event in America: Camp Bushido.

► Chuck Norris beats Ron Marchini by half a point to win the black-belt division at Tak Kubota's International Karate Federation Championship. His victory sets the stage for a possible rematch with Tonny Tulleners, who narrowly beat Norris earlier in the year at the California State Championship.

► The British Medical Association conducts a study that exonerates karate, which has been criticized for inciting youngsters who watch it on television.

► The 1966 East Coast Open Karate Tournament is a who's who of the martial arts in America. Gary Alexander directs, Maung Gyi acts as chief judge, and Peter Urban, S. Henry Cho, George Cofield and Johnny Pachivas serve as "participating judges."

► A reader from Georgia is a fan of the mixed martial arts and doesn't even know it. He writes: *"Boxing Illustrated* carried a story about how a boxer knocked out a judo expert with one punch in less than one minute in Yokohama, Japan, on January 12, 1928. I have always said a good boxer could whip a good judo player. But with a karate expert, it would be something else—he would be able to do away with either one."

World's Leading Magazine of Self-Defense.

BLACK BELT

OCTOBER 1966　　50 CENTS

KARATE'S

LITTLE KNOWN

WEAPON...

...The Mind as

Physical Force!

ISSUE THIRTY-FOUR | OCTOBER 1966

The 34th issue of *Black Belt* was dated October 1966. It was 66 pages long and featured a color painting of two *karateka* on the cover.

Vol. 4, No. 10, 50 cents

▶ In a letter to the editor, a reader describes what he claims is a virtually no-holds-barred tournament held annually in Formosa (now Taiwan): "In the Free Fight Olympiad ... exponents from any martial art may enter. Contact is allowed, with only the eyes, throat and groin being safe areas. Many times, fatal injuries result from combat." Anyone else skeptical?

▶ An enterprising individual named Jimmy S. Gozawa begins offering what has become an essential in the industry: *dojo* accident insurance.

▶ Californian Doug Holford trades in his Caltech textbooks for a *gi* and a thong as he journeys to Japan to experience karate and sumo wrestling firsthand.

▶ In "Tapping the Power of the Mind," karate great Tsutomu Ohshima reveals that *shotokan* founder Gichin Funakoshi never talked about *ki* energy.

▶ Subscribers can now buy any back issue of *Black Belt* for the princely sum of 60 cents.

▶ The Japanese martial arts are taking Burma by storm. After being introduced to judo, karate, *jujutsu, kendo* and *aikido,* the Burmese are apparently dissecting the moves and recombining them in what they hope are new and improved ways.

▶ Risei Kano, son of judo founder Jigoro Kano, tries—and fails—to make the first Asian Judo Championship a success. Eight countries send athletes, but none, to put it politely, is in any danger of being mistaken for the best of the best.

▶ Sumo champ Kitabayama retires from the sport. The reason: At 242 pounds, he's too small to handle up-and-coming behemoths.

▶ American Mike Anderson takes the helm of the German-Korean Karate Federation.

▶ Judo is the latest sport to be added to the list of endeavors approved by the President's Council on Physical Fitness.

▶ Ed Parker introduces the Makiwara-Waza Man, an angle-iron adversary that features seven strategically placed striking pads for the ultimate in realistic self-defense training. The deluxe model sells for a cool $49.50.

World's Leading Magazine of Self-Defense.

BLACK BELT

NOVEMBER 1966 ✕ VOL. IV, NO. 11   50 CENTS

REDISCOVERED...a hand-to-hand combat art used by the bodyguard of ancient Hawaiian Kings

ISSUE THIRTY-FIVE | NOVEMBER 1966

The 35th issue of *Black Belt* was dated November 1966. It was 66 pages long and featured a color painting of two Hawaiian wrestlers on the cover.

Vol. 4, No. 11, 50 cents

▶ *Black Belt* readers are up in arms over the previous issue's statement that boxers come from the "lower strata of our society and are anything but a good type." One man pens a rebuttal that focuses on attacking the whole martial arts industry: "Nowhere in any sport can you find as many outright liars, many claiming to be black belts, as in the martial arts."

▶ The karate- and judo-practicing mayor of Manila, Philippines, uses his empty-hand skills to disarm a pistol-packing punk.

▶ *Lua,* a rare Hawaiian style that's also known as the art of bone-breaking, is introduced to the American martial arts community via the cover story.

▶ Looked on as oddities in the Land of the Rising Sun, the grappling girls of Japan prove there's no such thing as the weaker sex when they work out at the Kodokan judo headquarters in Tokyo.

▶ Noting an increase in assaults perpetrated on young ladies, a California legislator launches a campaign to teach girls self-defense in school.

▶ An extra-wide black belt with the name of your art embroidered on it will set you back a whopping $2.65.

▶ Escorted by two Secret Service agents, John F. Kennedy Jr. attends a sumo tournament in Honolulu and chats with a champion named Taiho.

▶ Foreshadowing the current push toward gun control, some knee-jerk citizens of the Philippines react to a local karate murder by demanding that all martial arts students submit to registration. "It's high time for the government to consider seriously the truth that in the hands of an expert, karate or judo is as deadly as a loaded gun," the editor of the *Philippine Sun* writes.

▶ Tung Hu-ling, a renowned *tai chi* master from China, tours the United States to spread the internal art.

▶ Jesse Kuhaulua, a 280-pound ex-football player from Hawaii, ravages the Tokyo sumo scene with victory after victory, but Japanese pundits claim that the foreigner's weak legs will prevent him from reaching the top.

▶ The U.S. Food and Drug Administration cracks down on the Zen diet, a Japanese macrobiotic blend of natural foods that has been blamed for several American deaths.

▶ In a rare how-to article, Chuck Norris teaches one of his favorite *tang soo do* techniques: faking a front kick and scoring with a roundhouse.

World's Leading Magazine of Self-Defense.

BLACK BELT

DECEMBER 1966 ★ 50 CENTS

A legendary band of espionage
agents terrorized old Japan
with their sinister art of
Nin-jitsu, applying their
secrets to causes damned
and praised through history.

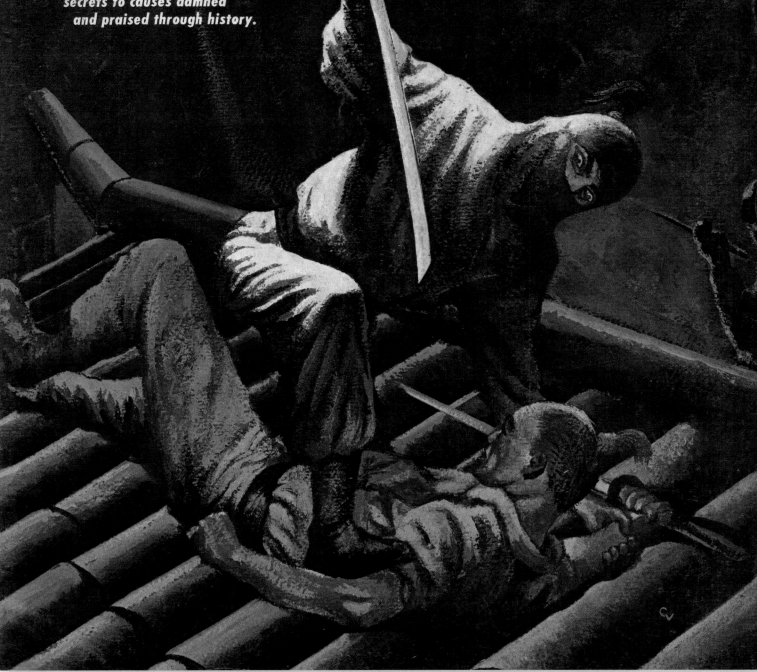

ISSUE THIRTY-SIX | DECEMBER 1966

The 36th issue of *Black Belt* was dated December 1966. It was 66 pages long and featured a color painting of two ninja warriors on the cover.

Vol. 4, No. 12, 50 cents

► In a subtle acknowledgment of the continuing advancement of martial arts technique around the world, the editor of *Black Belt* writes, "With the young men coming up in the arts today showing top speed, reflexes and conditioning, it is difficult for older men who are acting as referees to keep up with them."

► The country with the greatest number of martial arts practitioners outside of Asia is … France? Yup. The French Federation of Judo and Associated Arts has determined that the modest European nation hosts 93,000 licensed *judoka,* 6,000 licensed *karateka,* 2,500 licensed *aikidoka* and 1,000 active *savate* practitioners.

► In an article that questions the worth of the modern black belt, *kenpo* founder Ed Parker opines: "I don't think that rank is important at all. What is important is how much karate a student learns."

► *Black Belt* reports on the latest craze in the martial arts world: outdoor summer camps.

► Thomas LaPuppet is named grand champion of the first United Karate Federation Tournament in New York City.

► Decades before the art of the ninja would earn respect in the West, Japan correspondent Andy Adams writes: *"Ninjutsu* is the dark side of the Oriental martial arts. They moved stealthily as masked raiders, hired out as spies, arsonists, extortionists and even assassins to the great warring lords of feudal Japan."

► A medical doctor prescribes a healthy dose of judo as the cure for juvenile delinquency. "The physical experience of being slammed to the mat can serve several significant purposes," he claims. "These include the realization that … pain may be tolerated and further that pain is not so terrible that it must be avoided, even if avoidance involves a loss of self-esteem."

► An American construction company in Vietnam is trying to recruit 120 black belts to teach the fighting arts to its security guards. A cool $500 a month will be paid for services rendered.

► Wayne, New Jersey's lone policewoman is ordered to train in judo for 192 hours just like her male counterparts. Otherwise, she will be dropped from the force.

► Just in time for Christmas: A 14-inch-tall judo doll, complete with authentic uniform and a black belt, sells for $3.85.

World's Leading Magazine of Self-Defense

BLACK BELT

JANUARY, 1967

Okinawa's Karatemen —
Sticklers
for
conditioning

I S S U E   T H I R T Y - S E V E N | J A N U A R Y   1 9 6 7

The 37th issue of *Black Belt* was dated January 1967. It was 66 pages long and featured a color painting of a *karateka* pulverizing roof tiles on the cover.

Vol. 5, No. 1, 50 cents

▶ A Hawaiian karate expert travels to Hong Kong and experiences what we have seen movie martial artists endure for decades. "I had the hardest time just getting the master to talk to me," he says. "I went the first night, and he barely acknowledged my presence. I went the second night, and we talked some—but no instruction. The same on the third night. The master was testing me."

▶ A sentiment echoed throughout the history of the martial arts in America is voiced by an instructor from Indiana: To avoid complaints about officiating, all tournaments should draw on a national cadre of professional referees.

▶ When a mix-up causes Jhoon Rhee to confuse Skipper Mullins with Lewis Mullins in a tournament report, *Black Belt* replies: "Unfortunately, Mr. Rhee's English is at times about on a par with our Korean." Fast-forward 35 years, and you'll find that the talented *taekwondo* master is one of the most articulate members of the English-speaking martial arts community.

▶ A loyal reader writes to have his school added to *Black Belt's* Dojo Directory. His name? Gosei Yamaguchi.

▶ A youthful Masaaki Hatsumi, then known as Yoshiaki Hatsumi, is shown demonstrating a bamboo poison-water gun in a feature that reveals the secrets of *ninjutsu's* fantastic weaponry.

▶ *Black Belt* treads on holy ground with an article that describes the self-defense tactics used in ancient times. "Some of the most famous men mentioned in the Bible proved to be experts in various arts of self-defense," the author writes.

▶ An advertiser touts a veritable display case full of martial arts jewelry. Excluding the karate and judo lighters, the highest price for a single item is $2. (The lighters go for $6.50 apiece, in case you're wondering.)

▶ Negotiations are under way to launch a martial arts tour that will feature a series of America-vs.-Asia tournaments. Involved parties may include Tsutomu Ohshima, Jhoon Rhee, Ed Parker, Chuck Norris and Tonny Tulleners.

▶ The team from Wally Jay's martial arts club rakes in eight out of 13 division wins at the American Judo and Jujutsu Federation Tournament.

▶ Honolulu's Kenneth Funakoshi is promoted to third-degree black belt.

▶ Another perennial problem in the martial arts community is dragged into the *Black Belt* spotlight: "To hold a true world karate championship, all major organizations from major countries should have their best man compete," reader William Dometrich opines.

World's Leading Magazine of Self-Defense

BLACK BELT

FEBRUARY 1967   50 CENTS

Russia's Rugged Cossacks
and Siberian villagers help
develop SAMBO, a
free-wheeling sport of
self-defense now being
exported to Japan
and other countries.

ISSUE THIRTY-EIGHT | FEBRUARY 1967

The 38th issue of *Black Belt* was dated February 1967. It was 66 pages long and featured a color painting of burly Russian *sambo* players on the cover.

Vol. 5, No. 2, 50 cents

▶ Gosei Yamaguchi, son of *goju-ryu* founder Gogen Yamaguchi, contacts *Black Belt* to set the record straight: Despite what some have claimed, his famous father is not and has never been affiliated with an American karate organization.

▶ In the continuous battle between judo and karate, a reader writes in to argue that karate is inferior because "it is easier to punch and kick than to make a good judo technique." A rebuttal comes from another reader: "I like karate more than judo because it's tough. Remember what Mas Oyama said, 'Karate is for the rugged.' "

▶ In an article that introduces sambo to the Western world, Andy Adams writes: "Some Japanese judo men who have seen sambo in action claim that the Russian art is nothing but a wholesale takeover of judo—that about 75 percent of sambo techniques are really judo techniques. Actually, sambo is a grab-bag collection of [techniques from] all wrestling styles."

▶ A California insurance agent exposes the perils of practicing the martial arts. He says his company had to deal with 38 claims filed during its first five months of operation. The smallest claim was a whopping $5 and the largest was $500.

▶ *Black Belt* begins official distribution among secondary school students in the Philippines and female soldiers in the South Vietnamese army.

▶ *Ninjutsu* authority Masaaki Hatsumi, then known as Yoshiaki Hatsumi, reveals that he turned down an opportunity to serve as technical consultant for the James Bond blockbuster *You Only Live Twice.* His decision contrasts with the actions of a Japanese expert who reportedly hired himself out to a local department store to attract shoppers.

▶ Paul Maruyama wins the annual *Black Belt* scholarship and opts to spend his prize money studying judo at the Kodokan in Tokyo.

▶ After perusing a *Black Belt* report that criticized the officiating at his most recent karate event, Ed Parker unloads: "It would appear to me after reading your article that the tournament was equaled by the literary style of your story, which apparently was written either to please your readers, [thereby] inciting circulation and sales of your magazine so more people would know about karate, or to create a controversy that never existed."

▶ Chuck Norris teaches an old standby: the Korean interpretation of the spinning back kick.

▶ A peacenik from Akron, Ohio, complains about a recent cover painting that depicted Tsutomu Ohshima "clobbering" another *karateka* with a punch. "Gory pictures of this type tend to discourage potential karate students." If the writer is still alive and kicking, let's hope he hasn't seen the Ultimate Fighting Championship or the Sabaki Challenge.

World's Leading Magazine of Self-Defense

BLACK BELT

MARCH 1967 ⬡ 50 CENTS

SAVATE MAKES A COMEBACK—Famous foot-fighting system rose from the Paris underworld to become France's national art of self defense.

ISSUE THIRTY-NINE | MARCH 1967

The 39th issue of *Black Belt* was dated March 1967. It was 66 pages long and featured a color painting of a high-kicking *savate* practitioner on the cover.

Vol. 5, No. 3, 50 cents

▶ The reign of judo continues. Out of 82 books advertised on four pages, 50 focus on the Japanese grappling art.

▶ Robert Trias, director of the United States Karate Association, offers a solution to the refereeing problem that plagues tournaments: a nationwide series of clinics to be conducted by karate's leading masters.

▶ Then-editor Anthony DeLeonardis takes a snapshot of the state of martial arts fashion. Among his observations are a few comments about the infamous *hakama*. Ted Tabura, cover your ears.

▶ *Black Belt* introduces its readers to the French art of savate, which the staff nicknames "the manly art of self-defense."

▶ Martial artists around the world worry that a karate killing in England (seven blows landed in three seconds, fracturing six ribs, rupturing the liver, damaging the voice box and injuring the lungs) could lead to the arts' being outlawed there and in other countries.

▶ In an interview with 71-year-old judo pioneer Sego Murakami, the *sensei* reveals his art's Capitol Hill roots. "There was President Theodore Roosevelt, who took judo lessons in the White House from Yamashita, a 10th *dan*. Both Roosevelt and his daughter became *shodans*."

▶ Ninja legend Masaaki Hatsumi teaches the head butt and scissor grip—with the latter technique looking suspiciously like the Brazilian *jiu-jitsu* guard.

▶ A reader from Texas throws in the towel. "Well, I give up as many others have," he writes. "I hope to resume some day when the martial arts mature. The leading karate men are just not acting like true *budo* men. I hope *aikido* learns from karate's mistakes."

▶ Future *Black Belt* Hall of Fame member Thomas LaPuppet wins top honors in sparring at the Fifth Canadian Karate Championship.

▶ President Lyndon B. Johnson is treated to a *taekwondo* demonstration when he visit Seoul, South Korea.

▶ A French publisher is accused of bootlegging Mas Oyama's quintessential text, *This Is Karate*.

▶ In a move to unite all the martial arts taught within its borders, the Uruguay Judo Federation opens its ranks to bring karate and aikido practitioners into the fold.

▶ Because of unfamiliar rules, Chuck Norris is eliminated after his first match at the 1966 American Tang Soo Do Invitational Karate Tournament in Washington, D.C.

▶ In Covington, Kentucky, Lloyd Bridges is promoted to second *kyu* in *kushin kan* karate. Nah ... couldn't be.

World's Leading Magazine of Self-Defense

BLACK BELT

APRIL 1967   🅚   50 CENTS

VOL. V, NO. 4

ZEN ARCHERY
The Most Royal
of Japan's
18 Martial Arts

SPECIAL: U.S. Karate's Ten Top Tournament Players

ISSUE FORTY | APRIL 1967

T he 40th issue of *Black Belt* was dated April 1967. It was 66 pages long and featured a color painting of a mounted Japanese archer on the cover.

Vol. 5, No. 4, 50 cents

► In his editorial, the editor of *Black Belt* notes: "The American *judoka* is the quiet man of the martial arts. Karate is quite different. American karate men are not at all reluctant to fire off to us their viewpoints on a wide range of subjects." Things haven't changed much in the past three and a half decades.

► A college in the Philippines adds karate and judo to its offerings.

► Andy Adams, *Black Belt's* Asian correspondent, calls *kyudo* (traditional archery) the most royal of Japan's 18 martial arts. "The training and ideals it espouses helped shape the Japanese personality and character," he claims.

► The top-10 karate players in the United States are named: Joe Lewis, Steve Loring, Skipper Mullins, Chuck Norris, Allen Steen, Carlos Bunda, Thomas LaPuppet, Julio La Salle, Frank Smith and Tonny Tulleners.

► The entire judo team of Hungary is killed when a plane crashes in Czechoslovakia.

► Already a karate legend, Fumio Demura reveals the secrets of *shito-ryu* to an American audience. In Japan, he says, it is regarded as one of the big four subsets of the popular striking art. (The other three are *wado-ryu, goju-ryu* and *shotokan.)*

► The United States ramps up for an explosion of Japanese martial arts tournaments, including events that showcase kyudo, *kendo,* judo and karate. Sponsoring names include Chuck Norris, Ed Parker, Teruyuki Okazaki, Hidetake Nishiyama, Tsutomu Ohshima and Jhoon Rhee.

► After a gaggle of readers sound off on the controversial subject of *chi* energy, Peter Urban opines: "My personal opinion is that the entire question of chi is in the same category as UFOs. There are those who swear both ways in regard to their existence. I have decided to just continue collecting data and benefit from the accrued knowledge."

► The number of karate practitioners in the USA is estimated at 50,000.

► After noticing last month's feature on the French art of *savate,* a reader suggests a story about Col. William E. Fairbairn, the renowned hand-to-hand combat and knife-fighting expert of World War II fame. For some reason, the editorial staff does not appear to think much of the idea.

► Female members of the Norwegian army begin receiving judo and *jujutsu* training.

► The flood begins: Two readers write to inform the world that karate—or is it kung fu?—is now on television. Whatever the art is, the source is certain: Bruce Lee, who just started playing Kato on *The Green Hornet.*

World's Leading Magazine of Self-Defense

BLACK BELT

MAY 1967 50 CENTS

THE WORLD JUDO TOURNAMENT THAT FEW REALLY WANTED BEGINS TO PICK UP STEAM

Issue Forty-One | May 1967

T he 41st issue of *Black Belt* was dated May 1967. It was 66 pages long and featured a color painting of two *judoka* on the cover.

Vol. 5, No. 5, 50 cents

► In a letter, Spc. 5th Class Vic Usher writes, "Even with the war to contend with, a large number of GIs still find time for karate." Of course, he is speaking about military operations in Vietnam, not Iraq.

► *Black Belt* launches a massive undertaking: a survey of the state of the martial arts in America. Questionnaires are being mailed to 500 *dojo,* which the staff believes are the majority of training halls in the nation.

► *Black Belt* correspondent Andy Adams reveals a morsel of truth about the martial arts of the East versus those of the West: "One criticism that has been made of *kyudo* is that while it may be a good philosophy, it does not necessarily make for good shooting. Today, for instance, it is American archery which is considered to be the best—or the most accurate—in the world."

► In an essay about the legendary Hohan Soken and the rare white-swan form of Okinawan karate, a *Black Belt* writer claims that although the teachings are cloaked in secrecy, a few tidbits are beginning to leak out: "*Chi* is the single most emphasized element of this technique, and mastery of it is essential."

► After judo is ejected from the lineup for the 1972 Olympics, a campaign gets under way in Europe to have it added to the Winter Games.

► Signaling an end to Japan's dominance of martial arts news in America, Korea emerges from its information isolation. Among the relevant reports are a story about Korean *yudo* practitioners heading to Vietnam for a demonstration tour, a piece about *taekwondo's* incursion into Yugoslavia, a news item about a team of Korean taekwondo practitioners' plan to compete against teams from several Japanese universities, and mention of Taiwan's official request that the South Korean government dispatch more instructors to the island nation.

► The battle over the origin of martial arts techniques rages. A reader from Coopersburg, Pennsylvania, says, "I have some prints of medieval European [art] showing 'judo' throws at least 300 years old that will make a lot of romantic *budoka* wince."

► Japan's sumo grand champion retires—and collects a cool $21,000. It is the highest monetary award ever given to a competitor in the traditional sport.

► Langley Air Force Base in Hampton, Virginia, inaugurates a new martial arts program. It is composed of techniques from judo, karate and *aikido.*

World's Leading Magazine of Self-Defense

BLACK BELT

1st NORTH AMERICAN KARATE CHAMPIONSHIP

JUNE 1967   50 CENTS

CALIFORNIA'S CHUCK NORRIS WINS A ONE-OF-A-KIND "TOURNAMENT OF CHAMPIONS"

ISSUE FORTY-TWO | JUNE 1967

The 42nd issue of *Black Belt* was dated June 1967. It was 66 pages long and featured a color painting of rising star Chuck Norris on the cover.

Vol. 5, No. 6 , 50 cents

▶ Chuck Norris rebounds after losing to Bob Engle and defeats Joe Lewis to take top honors at S. Henry Cho's Tournament of Champions in New York City. Skipper Mullins comes in third.

▶ A 22-year-old Hawaiian grappler by the name of Jesse Kuhaulua upsets the apple cart in Japan by becoming the first foreigner to win his way into the high ranks of sumo. His weight: a respectable 280 pounds.

▶ In a rant about a recent TV show designed to bring karate and judo to the American public, one reader writes: "An excellent program could have [resulted] with Tak Kubota demonstrating his ability and Chuck Norris demonstrating his knife technique. But instead, what did they show? One girl besting five men with an umbrella." Another reader chimes in on the lack of realism: "The young lady who was supposedly defending herself against five men did not take them on simultaneously. Even a high-ranked black belt would be hard-pressed to defend himself against five attackers if all were attacking as one."

▶ Future *Black Belt* Hall of Fame member Ki Whang Kim opens a chain of East Coast schools that teach *tang soo do* and *aikido*.

▶ The Philippines boasts a whopping three people who possess a black belt in judo.

▶ A European journalist reports on Swiss Alp wrestling, an indigenous grappling system that bears a striking resemblance to judo and sumo.

▶ In a review of Georges Sylvain's *Scientific Method of Police Fighting,* Dr. Philip J. Rasch rips its brutality: "On page 39, the author recommends that after having forced the man to the ground, you should 'fall full-force onto his ribs with your knee.' " Kind of tame by today's standards, isn't it?

▶ After an absence of more than 10 years, *taekwondo* legend Jhoon Rhee visits his native Korea and meets with his instructor, Ohm Un-kyu.

▶ Paving the way for a steady stream of career-swapping martial artists, Japanese judo champ Seiji Sakaguchi retires from competition to join the American pro-wrestling circuit.

▶ South Korean soldiers erect a taekwondo gymnasium in South Vietnam, where the kicking art is all the rage for more than 10,000 practitioners.

World's Leading Magazine of Self-Defense

BLACK BELT

JULY 1967 **K** 50 CENTS

THE
"GRAND ULTIMATE FIST"

China's Tai Chi Chuan is the oldest and most widely practiced of any form of boxing today

ISSUE FORTY-THREE | JULY 1967

T he 43rd issue of *Black Belt* was dated July 1967. It was 66 pages long and featured a color painting of two *tai chi chuan* practitioners on the cover.

Vol. 5, No. 7, 50 cents

▶ An 18-year-old karate white belt named Danny Stewart is killed during the California State Championships. Reports indicate that he was suffering from mononucleosis and should not have been allowed to compete. The cause of death is listed as a ruptured spleen resulting from blows to the stomach.

▶ In response to a *Black Belt* article about *chi,* a reader from Chicago hypothesizes that the mystical form of internal energy may have been the basis for biblical references to laying-on-of-hands healing methods.

▶ The best techniques of karate are taught in a new 8mm film set. More than two hours of instruction by experts from the Japan Karate Association will set you back $60.

▶ In "The Grand Ultimate Fist of Tai Chi Chuan," the author states: "The art can be studied for physical exercise and health alone, in which case it is referred to as tai chi. A smaller proportion of the population engages in the self-defense system, which is called tai chi chuan."

▶ Under the leadership of Risei Kano, son of Jigoro Kano, judo experiences growing pains. "In a sense, it has outgrown Japan," Andy Adams writes. "It has become a world sport."

▶ "The Art That Couldn't Be Banned" tells the tale of the Filipinos who fought against the Spanish and their effort to extinguish *arnis.*

▶ In the early days of the martial arts in Hawaii, judo and *jujutsu* join forces to combat what some practitioners perceive as a sumo invasion. We all know which team won.

▶ Tokyo University of Education prepares to launch a *budo* course. Previously, no government-run institution has been allowed to teach the martial arts.

▶ The first karate tournament is held in Malaysia. More than 100 men and women show up to trade blows.

▶ A kinder, gentler Japanese police force is taught that the public should not automatically be viewed as the enemy. Cops will soon update their self-defense training with more karate and *aikido* and less judo.

▶ Veronica and Angela Cartwright are the first students to enroll at the Sherman Oaks Karate Studio, which Joe Lewis and Bob Wall operate in Southern California. Veronica would go on to co-star in *Alien,* and Angela would continue to play Penny Robinson in the *Lost in Space* TV series until 1968.

World's Leading Magazine of Self-Defense

BLACK BELT

AUGUST 1967

50 CENTS

007
adopts an arsenal
of Oriental
self-defense
arts for
YOU ONLY LIVE TWICE'

U.S. JUDO
CHAMPIONSHIPS
fail to draw a
crowd in Las Vegas

ISSUE FORTY-FOUR | AUGUST 1967

The 44th issue of *Black Belt* was dated August 1967. It was 66 pages long and featured a color photo of Sean Connery on the cover.

Vol. 5, No. 8, 50 cents

► When asked about life after his recent retirement from competition, Chuck Norris replies: "I've never been so pestered in my life. Everyone has been after me to change my mind about quitting. I keep getting letters and telephone calls from across the country from *sensei* who want me to compete in their tournaments."

► A Rhode Island lawmaker introduces a bill to make any assault in which the martial arts are used a felony punishable by up to 10 years in prison.

► An African-American martial artist writes in search of information about training halls in Atlanta because the only one he can find is segregated.

► The editor of *Black Belt* decries the state of judo in America: "The U.S. Judo Federation is made up almost exclusively of old men from Japan who have been running U.S. judo the way they like it for years."

► The cover story describes the plethora of martial arts mayhem audiences will be treated to in *You Only Live Twice,* the newest 007 adventure, which takes place mostly in Japan. Before filming, star Sean Connery underwent a crash course in the combat arts from Donn F. Draeger and received an honorary third-degree black belt from Mas Oyama.

► A reader reports on his encounter at a Detroit *tang soo do* school run by Sang Kyu Shim: "I asked him why I had never seen him in *Black Belt* or his students in competitions. He only smiled and said, 'Too busy training.' "

► *Black Belt* presents its annual scholarship award to Howard Fish Jr. and donates a cool grand to the World Judo Fund.

► A self-proclaimed "judo-girl with five years of experience" insists that most women take up the grappling art to "develop a trim, healthy body and to acquire grace of movement—not to learn how to defeat somebody else."

► The martial arts community unites against a tournament the World Karate Federation plans to stage in Chicago. Why? The organization's head, John Keehan, has been arrested on charges of trying to bomb a competitor's *dojo*.

► Allen H. Good, president of the International Institute of Self-Defense in New Jersey, announces to the world that no one under 15 should be allowed to study karate.

► Myoung Kwan-sik, an official with the Korea Hapkido Association, claims his art is more popular than any other style in South Korea.

► Shannon Heft is selected as the 1967 International Karate Queen. Perhaps that's a tradition the martial arts world needs to resurrect.

World's Leading Magazine of Self-Defense

BLACK BELT

SEPTEMBER 1967 ⍰ 50 CENTS

RUGGED JOE LEWIS WINS FIRST LEG OF KARATE'S "TRIPLE CROWN"

TEN U.S. JUDO HOPEFULS TO KEEP AN EYE ON FOR WORLD CHAMPIONSHIPS

ISSUE FORTY-FIVE | SEPTEMBER 1967

The 45th issue of *Black Belt* was dated September 1967. It was 66 pages long and featured a color photo of Joe Lewis on the cover.

Vol. 5, No. 9, 50 cents

▶ The lead story: *Black Belt* expands. The world's leading magazine of self-defense gets a makeover and brings a bunch of foreign correspondents on board. Its parent company also launches a travel periodical titled *Asian Adventure*.

▶ The mighty Joe Lewis, 22, wins the Jhoon Rhee National Championship, one of the three largest karate events in the United States. He has reportedly abandoned his bad-boy persona.

▶ One of *Black Belt's* historians examines the life of the legendary Miyamoto Musashi. Film buffs learn that his exploits were recorded in 1956's Oscar-winning *Samurai*.

▶ Isao Okano becomes the smallest man to win the All-Japan Judo Championship. He tips the scale at a scant 176 pounds.

▶ The editor of *Black Belt* takes Hayward Nishioka to task for not winning in judo as much as he used to: "They argue that he is even better than two years ago but that he has just not been trying as hard. The good-looking Nishioka, who tools around Southern California in his [Jaguar] XKE sports car, needs an added incentive to compete."

▶ If you're under 5 feet 4 inches tall, you can snag a double-weave judo *gi* for the tidy sum of $10.50.

▶ Andy Adams, the magazine's correspondent in the Land of the Rising Sun, reports on the scandalous proposal to allow foreigners to enter the All-Japan Karate Championships.

▶ In response to the recent death of a tournament competitor, a karate instructor in Gainesville, Florida, proposes requiring all martial arts students to undergo a medical checkup before joining a *dojo* and at least once a year afterward. These days, it wouldn't be long before such a regulation resulted in a lawsuit.

▶ A judo-practicing woman in London becomes the subject of a restraining order after violently throwing her hubby to the ground. He winds up in a nursing home, and she winds up divorced.

▶ *Bersilat,* Malaysia's homegrown art of self-defense, is introduced to the Western world.

▶ A Syracuse, New York-based woman witnesses a bout of female sparring at a karate tournament in Washington, D.C. "It was street fighting at its best," she says, "with scratching, hair-pulling and face-slapping the favorite techniques." Organizer Jhoon Rhee reportedly remarks, "Now we know why they don't draft women—they're too vicious."

World's Leading Magazine of Self-Defense

OCTOBER 1967 50 CENTS

BLACK BELT

BLACK BELT SURVEY: U.S. Karate Forges Ahead Of Judo

HOW EFFECTIVE IS JUDO IN POLICE WORK?

GREEN HORNET'S "KATO"
Does He Really
Practice Kung-Fu?

Issue Forty-Six | October 1967

The 46th issue of *Black Belt* was dated October 1967. It was 66 pages long and featured a black-and-white photo of Bruce Lee as the main cover image.

Vol. 5, No. 10, 50 cents

► Mostly because of his hugely popular portrayal of Kato in *The Green Hornet*, Bruce Lee appears on his first *Black Belt* cover. However, to placate a readership raised on hard Japanese karate and judo, the article sets out to determine whether Lee's version of *gung fu* is realistic.

► A reader from New York reveals an important part of Lee's appeal: "He teaches gung fu to anyone in spite of race, creed or nationality."

► Fed up with seemingly every student in the nation practicing a different set of forms, the Korea Taekwondo Association decides to unify the art's *poomsae*. It has approved nine so far.

► Shades of things to come: A ballet dancer in England signs up for judo lessons and breaks his arm during his first class, then promptly sues his instructor. He is awarded 5,500 pounds.

► Vietnam appeals to KTA former chairman Choi Hong-hi to get Korea to send more *taekwondo* instructors to tutor its police force.

► Rio de Janeiro, Brazil, bans kids under 14 from practicing karate.

► In Korea, a 25-year-old third-degree *tang soo do* black belt is arrested for killing a troublesome drunk with a knife-hand strike to the back of the neck.

► *Black Belt* finishes its first survey of the martial arts in America and finds that at the end of 1966, there were 113,000 *karateka* and 75,000 *judoka*. The Japanese arts dominate, with Korea in second place and Okinawa in third. The Chinese arts are expected to climb quickly because of the boost expected from Lee.

► In 1966 the average student-to-teacher ratio was as follows: 71 to 1 for the Japanese arts, 58 to 1 for the Okinawan arts, 57 to 1 for the Korean arts and 36 to 1 for the Chinese arts.

► Chuck Norris comes out of retirement for a rematch with Joe Lewis at the All-American Open Karate Championship. Norris lands a side kick to Lewis' gut and walks away with the grand champion title.

► After a rough-and-tumble tour of Japan, a group of American martial artists concludes that the Westerners hold the edge in power but that the Easterners are better technically.

► In an unforgivably ignorant appraisal of the karate tournament that hosted the aforementioned Norris-Lewis bout, *The New York Times* reports, "The players wore 'happy coats' tied with belts over pants that looked like mini-pajamas."

World's Leading Magazine of Self-Defense

BLACK BELT

NOVEMBER 1967 • 50 CENTS

"INSTANT ACTION"
IN KATO'S GUNG-FU

AIKIDOMAN SUFFERS
72 HOURS OF TORTURE

CHUCK NORRIS
CAPTURES KARATE'S
"TRIPLE CROWN"

SALT LAKE SETTLES
JUDO'S BIG RIDDLE...

...Fifth World Tournament Produces The Answer

ISSUE FORTY-SEVEN | NOVEMBER 1967

The 47th issue of *Black Belt* was dated November 1967. It was 66 pages long and featured a black-and-white photo of Mitsuo Matsunaga on the cover.

Vol. 5, No. 11, 50 cents

► A dedicated martial artist and loyal reader goes on the record: "I think *Black Belt* has become more interesting, and it should be a 'must' in every home around the globe. It is so educational and historical, and a great joy to read." The author of the letter? A renowned and respected master of the Indonesian martial arts named Willem de Thouars.

► Need a *bo?* An 8-foot-long white oak model goes for $10.50.

► Police officers in Europe congregate in Interlaken, Switzerland, for a crash course in judo and *jujutsu.*

► Police in Borneo apparently have a different attitude toward the martial arts. The commissioner reportedly has concerns that karate will turn boys and girls into deadly weapons. He views the locally grown art of *silat,* however, as perfectly OK.

► A reader from Arlington, California, writes to bemoan the state of the public's attitude toward the martial arts—which he blames on television. "The hero on TV is young, handsome and popular with the girls. When he meets bad guys, he just shows off his karate or judo. ... It would be a shame if the martial arts became a showoff sport."

► Ron Marchini takes first at the Pacific Coast Invitational Karate Tournament in San Francisco. Joe Lewis places third.

► On a break from his rise to superstardom, Bruce Lee demonstrates *gung fu* at the International Karate Championships, Ed Parker's Long Beach, California, event. His prowess wows the audience, but he doesn't overshadow the fighters—especially Chuck Norris, who takes top honors.

► For those who need a reminder of how far racial equality has come in less than four decades, Harold W. Reeves of Grand Rapids, Michigan, weighs in on the subject of masters who will not teach anyone who is not of their race: "Well, I am a Negro, which makes no difference at all. My color will not stop me from becoming interested in *tai chi chuan.* Nothing is impossible for me to learn."

► Choi Hong-hi's 304-page seminal text, *Taekwon-Do: The Art of Self-Defence,* is released for $7.50.

► A clever *karateka* from Cajun Country composes a cute communiqué: "I have perfected the art of ... self-defense. It depends on liberating the force of *fumo,* that mysterious and elusive power that resides within the human body and animals, as well. The attainment of fumo is simple. Cease at once all efforts at personal hygiene. Diet is immaterial, but lean strongly toward beans, onions and garlic. Within days, you will feel the power of fumo emanating from you. Employ it in such moves as the single- or double-armpit exposure or in various other exposures too intimate to be discussed here. It is more than a method of self-defense. It is a way of life."

DECEMBER 1967 ✖ 50 CENTS

WORLD'S LEADING MAGAZINE OF SELF-DEFENSE

BLACK BELT

KARATE WEAPONS?
Use of the unknown sai
is finally revealed

"THE WAY" OF
THE SWORDSMAN
A samurai learns
the power of the mind

U.S. JUDO TEAM
DEFEATS ITSELF
in the
5th World Tourney!

*FUMIO DEMURA DEMONSTRATES
THE SAI TECHNIQUES*

ISSUE FORTY-EIGHT | DECEMBER 1967

The 48th issue of *Black Belt* was dated December 1967. It was 66 pages long and featured a black-and-white photo of Fumio Demura on the cover.

Vol. 5, No. 12, 50 cents

▶ A 29-year-old Israeli soldier who holds a black belt in karate and judo delivers two knifehand strikes to the neck of an armed Arab infiltrator. The man later dies from his injuries.

▶ Karate legend Mike Stone recounts his adventurous past: "About a year ago, someone wanted to see if I was strong enough to wrestle a lion or a tiger because the panther [is part of] our school insignia. I accepted the dare and went to Jungleland where they train wild animals for Tarzan movies. I took on a big, snarling, ferocious leopard in a grappling match. The big cat gave me a good mauling, scratching my face and arms, and I was mighty lucky to come out alive."

▶ Future reality-fighting pioneer Bradley Steiner pens a letter to thank *Black Belt* for covering the martial arts training of the U.S. Marines and encourages the staff to reveal the regimen of the Green Berets.

▶ Fumio Demura introduces Westerners to the mysterious world of the karate *sai*.

▶ Aaron Banks hosts the All-Martial Arts Show in New York City. "I believe that public interest is not just in tournaments but also in the arts themselves," he tells reporters. Thirty-seven years later, Banks is still serving up the Asian arts to a hungry public in the Big Apple.

▶ Kim Pyung-soo, *Black Belt's* correspondent in Korea, profiles his nation's Yudo Dae Hak, or Judo University. The faculty includes 10 professors, 15 lecturers and seven assistant professors. An estimated 300,000 Koreans are active in the martial sport.

▶ A reader from Minneapolis chastises *Black Belt* for criticizing competitors who use excessive force in the ring and then publicizing those who win by ignoring the rules regarding contact.

▶ Japanese *judoka* clean house at the 1967 Universiade by taking all six gold medals. South Korea claims all six silvers. Meanwhile, Howard Fish Jr., recipient of the *Black Belt* scholarship, bags a bronze.

▶ William J. Hatton of Las Vegas notes that the pageantry that goes hand in hand with martial arts practice in America is a uniquely American thing. "In Asia ... students wear such clothing as is customary for ordinary people engaging in normal industrial or agricultural activities," he insists.

▶ In all of Australia, only 150 people hold a black belt in judo.

▶ In one of the earliest documented uses of the term "grandmaster" within the martial arts world, F.H. Ruffra of Santa Monica, California, innocently states: "In a chess tournament, Chuck Norris would be the grandmaster, having bested his peers in the master class." Little could he know how the title would catch on.

WORLD'S LEADING MAGAZINE OF SELF-DEFENSE

BLACK BELT

JANUARY 1968 ⬡ 50 CENTS

HOWARD FISH
"One Man Team" Salvages U.S. Judo Image Abroad

OKINAWAN KARATE WEAPONS EXPERT
Simplifies Use Of The Sai

ZEN —Is It Necessary In The Martial Arts?

ISSUE FORTY-NINE | JANUARY 1968

T he 49th issue of *Black Belt* was dated January 1968. It was 66 pages long and featured a black-and-white photo of meditating monks on the cover.

Vol. 6, No. 1, 50 cents

▶ After scores of readers tear into the subject of Bruce Lee's legitimacy, which was discussed in last month's cover story, the "Little Dragon" responds in print with his usual eloquence and veracity.

▶ Andy Adams, *Black Belt's* Japan correspondent, examines the contention that Zen training is required for a person to advance to the highest levels of the martial arts.

▶ From the pen of a disgruntled reader: "The fact that, since the founding of your magazine, you have neglected to bring recognition to William K.S. Chow, 15th degree, illustrates what a farce your outfit really is."

▶ A martial artist who also happens to be a member of the Hell's Angels offers some sage advice on street survival: "A good *karateka* will always be someplace else when the fighting occurs."

▶ The British Overseas Airway Corporation advertises a 19-day vacation dubbed Bachelor's Orient. It promises, among other things, to take in "less-than-modest floor shows."

▶ Talk about luck! Tournament champ Joe Lewis begins instructing 25 women from the Hollywood Playboy Club at his Sherman Oaks Karate Studio.

▶ Waxing historical, *Black Belt* looks at Cornish wrestling and notes the many similarities it shares with judo.

▶ In a monumental upset, an American team defeats the champs of the All-Japan Collegiate Karate Federation in a Tokyo competition.

▶ In a review of Mas Oyama's rewritten *What Is Karate?,* Dr. Philip J. Rasch opines: "The book seems to emphasize all the rougher, sadistic sides of karate." Copies are available today on eBay.

▶ Eighteen-year-old Beverly Irene Branson becomes the first woman to demonstrate karate-based self-defense routines in the talent portion of a beauty pageant. After disarming mock assailants and thumping thugs, she wins the contest.

▶ A reader from Youngstown, Ohio, writes: "It is a mistake to believe Jigoro Kano had a better style of *jujutsu* (judo) than was practiced. The truth is, he was a better man. It is not the style, but the man behind it, that counts." It's a sentiment with which most 21st century fans of the mixed martial arts would agree.

WORLD'S LEADING MAGAZINE OF SELF-DEFENSE

BLACK BELT

FEBRUARY 1968 K 50 CENTS

THE MARTIAL ARTS IN RED CHINA TODAY

New Directions for the Old Arts of Tai Chi Chuan, Kung-fu, Pa-kua and Other Karate Forerunners

ANOTHER GEESINK BIDS FOR WORLD JUDO TITLE

THEY DIED FOR HONOR

The strange tale of Japan's famous 47 ronins

ISSUE FIFTY | FEBRUARY 1968

The 50th issue of *Black Belt* was dated February 1968. It was 66 pages long and featured a composite photo of nine Chinese-language martial arts books on the cover.

Vol. 6, No. 2, 50 cents

▶ A martial artist from San Francisco writes a letter to Bruce Lee: "Recently I witnessed a Chinese master break a chopstick by jamming it against his own throat. Furthermore, he picked up a hammer and hit himself all over. Later, he told the audience this is *chi*." Lee responds: "Why did he break the chopstick himself? Why didn't he invite someone else to jam it against his throat? Why did he not invite someone to come out and smash him with the hammer if the object is to show he can withstand pain? If *gung fu* consists of the above, the end of the art is arriving."

▶ George Dillman wrestles a 350-pound black bear named "Victor the Great." The bruin's track record has him pinning all his human opponents in less than five minutes each, but it takes the animal 20 minutes to conquer the future *Black Belt* Hall of Fame member.

▶ In a cover story about the newest fad in the martial arts community—the many styles of kung fu—the editor of *Black Belt* writes: "The Chinese fighting arts would certainly have to be called more sophisticated perhaps than the [Japanese and Korean arts]. They have developed out of the world's oldest culture."

▶ After losing a karate bout to Joe Lewis in 1967, Paul Pelela stages a comeback and defeats the fighting legend in a Seattle rematch.

▶ An Australian reader daringly commits his opinions about *Black Belt* to paper: "The biggest laugh is the Instructor Profile. I find it hard to believe that any true *judoka* would advertise himself. Americans, of course, are well-known for their attitude of self-praise and flamboyant behavior."

▶ After living in Japan for 15 years, *chung do kwan taekwondo* founder Lee Won-kuk returns to South Korea to teach his beloved art.

▶ The judo world waits with bated breath for the career of 18-year-old Gerard Geesink, baby brother of grappling-legend Anton Geesink, to take off.

▶ Yoshio Nanbu introduces *shito-ryu* karate to Europe. The obscure art is taught by only a handful of instructors outside Japan—including, of course, Fumio Demura in the United States.

▶ Need a black belt embroidered with gold-colored Chinese characters? It'll set you back a paltry $2.65. Add 10 cents for a size 4 and 30 cents for a size 5.

ISSUE FIFTY-ONE | MARCH 1968

The 51st issue of *Black Belt* was dated March 1968. It was 66 pages long and featured a photo of Robert Sluder, the Los Angeles Police Department's officer in charge of recruit training, on the cover.

Vol. 6, No. 3, 50 cents

▶ *Black Belt's* Japan correspondent writes, "Since the golden age of *jujutsu* 100 years ago, this ancient martial art has steadily declined. Today, it is in danger of complete extinction." He notes, however, that a watered-down version of the art that has forgone all "dangerous techniques" is enjoying unprecedented popularity in Japan.

▶ Vice President Hubert Humphrey is treated to a *taekwondo* demonstration by South Korean soldiers while visiting the Asian nation.

▶ In his cover story, Dan Rickey writes, "The almost complete lack of respect for law and order existing today in the United States seems to usher in a new set of morals and mores." Sound familiar? He then describes how police officers are being trained to use their batons in a way that is "much less offensive to the public ... with a thrust or jab to vulnerable points on the body."

▶ Among the LAPD officers highlighted in the article is *Black Belt's* own Bob Koga. He was later featured in our May 2002 issue, and his *Practical Aiki-Do* video and DVD series remains a best-seller.

▶ Jim Bregman, a bronze-medal winner at the 1964 Tokyo Olympics, proclaims: "I see no progress in American judo since the 1930s. It is in a deplorable state."

▶ At the 2nd American Tang Soo Do Invitational Tournament in Washington, D.C., Chuck Norris walks home with the grand championship. Mitchell Bobrow, the man who would later found a clothing company called Otomix, placed third in the heavyweight division.

▶ Chile boasts more than 1,500 active karate practitioners.

▶ At Fumio Demura's First Invitational Karate Tournament in Irvine, California, Tonny Tulleners takes top honors in sparring.

▶ Want to learn kung fu the high-tech way? You can buy your very own 200-foot-long 8mm instructional film for $39.95.

▶ Bruce Lee, Chuck Norris and Fumio Demura are among the masters who demonstrate at Tak Kubota's 3rd Annual Invitational Karate Tournament in Hollywood.

▶ According to an internal survey, the top-10 best-selling martial arts books of 1967 were (in descending order) *Dynamic Karate* by M. Nakayama, *Chinese Leg Maneuvers* by L. Uing-arng, *Taekwondo* by Choi Hong-hi, *Karate: Art of Empty-Hand Fighting* by H. Nishiyama, *Manual of Karate* by E.J. Harrison, *Pa-Kua* by R.W. Smith, *This Is Karate* by M. Oyama, *Aikido* by K. Uyeshiba, *Tai Chi Chuan* by Y.K. Chen and *What Is Karate?* by Oyama.

WORLD'S LEADING MAGAZINE OF SELF-DEFENSE   APRIL 1968   50 CENTS

BLACK BELT

► **HAWAIIAN GIANT STUNS JAPANESE SUMO WORLD!**

► How Dominant is Karate in Okinawa Today?

► Police Multiple Hand-to-Hand Techniques

Former Football Player, Jesse Kauhaulua, Makes a Big Splash in Sumo.

ISSUE FIFTY-TWO | APRIL 1968

The 52nd issue of *Black Belt* was dated April 1968. It was 66 pages long and featured a color photo of American-born sumo champion Jesse Kuhaulua, written as Kauhaulua on the cover.

Vol. 6, No. 4, 50 cents

▶ Presaging one of the biggest issues for 21st-century martial artists, a police officer writes: "A problem existing today is the segregation of the combat karatemen from the sport karatemen. Sport techniques are mostly scoped for the shoulder to the groin. Speed and deception are of prime importance. Combat techniques are scoped heavily to the head and below the waist, as most of the vital points are in these areas."

▶ Just 23 years after the end of World War II, during which the Japanese occupied the Korean peninsula, a team of four South Korean *taekwondo* experts performs on Japanese television. The Korea Taekwondo Association hopes it will open the doors to sending instructors to the neighboring nation.

▶ The number of *judoka* who regularly roll around in Germany tops 40,000.

▶ On the opposite side of the world in Okinawa, approximately 15,000 people practice karate. "Eighty percent of the men there have at one time or another studied karate," claims a master named Santos Kina.

▶ A reader from New Haven, Connecticut, opines: "I've been to quite a few tournaments, mostly Korean-style, and they make karate look like a joke. These men wouldn't last a second with one of the Japan Karate Association's first-degree black belts. ... The only worthwhile champ I've seen is Chuck Norris."

▶ In response to the number of reader requests to be connected with pen pals, *Black Belt* launches a new department dedicated to mail matchmaking.

▶ More than 3,300 karate enthusiasts brave the pouring rain for a chance to glimpse *goju* karate headmaster Gogen Yamaguchi at the U.S. Goju-Kai Championship in San Francisco. The highlight of his time on stage is a session of free sparring with his 32-year-old son, Gosei.

▶ Once a football star in Hawaii, Jesse Kuhaulua is living the high life in Tokyo, where his 10-5 record has lofted him to the upper echelon of sumo wrestling. "A cauliflower ear adds the mark of battle to his rugged good looks," Andy Adams writes. "His rough and ready appearance has been catnip to the local felines." Ah, the fringe benefits of martial arts stardom.

WORLD'S LEADING MAGAZINE OF SELF-DEFENSE   MAY 1968   50 CENTS

BLACK BELT

GREEN BERET TERROR: They kill at a rate of six to one

HEROES OF INTERPOL: Japanese police and martial arts

GUNG-FU AND THE TONGS: The 'Frisco warlords' revenge

Morihei Uyeshiba:
Mind-Power
Moves Mountains

ISSUE FIFTY-THREE | MAY 1968

The 53rd issue of *Black Belt* was dated May 1968. It was 66 pages long and featured a black-and-white photo of *aikido*'s Morihei Uyeshiba on the cover.

Vol. 6, No. 5, 50 cents

▶ *Black Belt* announces that it will sponsor the First International Convention of the Martial Arts to improve communication between instructors and promote the arts. A banquet featuring the newly born *Black Belt* Hall of Fame will take place the same weekend, as will the screening of martial arts films.

▶ At a round-table discussion hosted by *Black Belt,* Chuck Norris and Ed Parker are asked how long a student should train before being allowed to compete. "I would say about a year for most of them," Parker opines. Norris adds, "Some guys make it in nine months."

▶ Ed Parker beats 'em all to the punch: He's offering two 50-foot reels of instructional movie film for $5.99 postpaid.

▶ Kim Pyung-soo, *Black Belt's* Korea correspondent, is scheduled to launch a U.S. tour designed to teach Americans the new *taekwondo* forms.

▶ A Bruce Lee-worshipping reader from Brownsville, Pennsylvania, writes: "I know you do not know when *Tao of Jeet Kune Do* will be published, but as soon as you do, please print something about it. It will probably be a sellout." Editor's note for 2008: The quintessential text is now in its 60st printing—that's more than 1 million copies sold, folks.

▶ Lawmen at the first Asian Interpol Conference conclude that the plunging crime rate in Japan can be attributed to the police officers' knowledge of karate and judo.

▶ Eighty-five-year-old Morihei Uyeshiba is still making a name for himself in Japan with displays of aikido that would bring acclaim to a man half his age. In one, the founder of the evasive art bests a string of strapping young bucks in front of the Foreign Correspondents Club in Tokyo.

▶ Foreshadowing the fighting fad of the 2000s—the rise of the reality-based martial arts—*Black Belt* profiles the training and techniques of the Green Berets. "It is safer to go in and fight than [it is to] hide behind cover," the author writes.

▶ A soldier stationed in the Far East writes, "I was in Korea before coming to Vietnam, and my instructors in taekwondo couldn't wait for my issues of *Black Belt* to arrive. When I showed them your fine magazine, they would go off in a world of their own and solemnly work on the [techniques]."

▶ Want a one-year subscription to *Black Belt?* It'll set you back a fin. (That's $5 to all you youngsters out there.)

WORLD'S LEADING MAGAZINE OF SELF-DEFENSE

JUNE 1968 50 CENTS

BLACK BELT

- ▶ **IMPERIAL GUARDS:** The tough martial arts machine of Japan
- ▶ **TYRANTS OF THE TONGS:** The Chinatown Squad's open war
- ▶ **THE CAUSE OF KARATE:** Jhoon Rhee makes karate big business
- ▶ **THE EAST VS. WEST KARATE TOURNAMENT:** A muddled melee

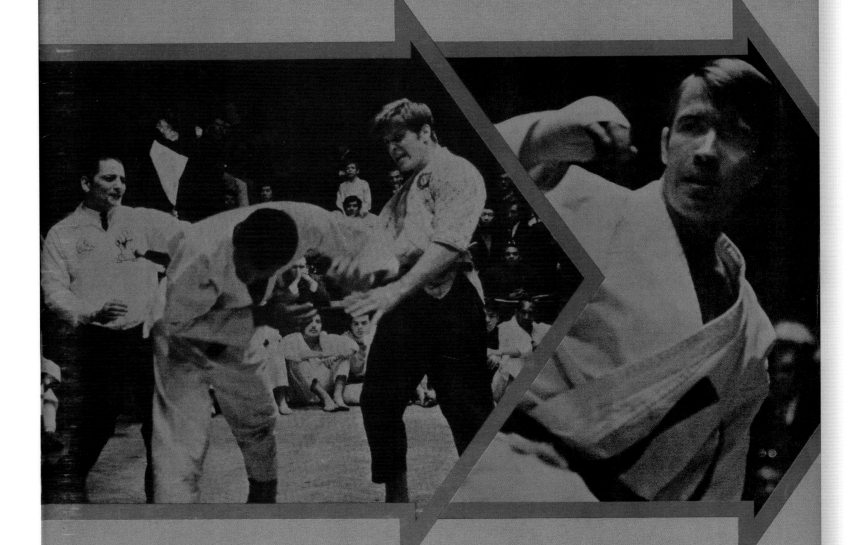

New heroes emerged while old hero Chuck Norris (r), tasted defeat in New York tourney.

ISSUE FIFTY-FOUR | JUNE 1968

The 54th issue of *Black Belt* was dated June 1968. It was 66 pages long and featured a bevy of legends on the cover: (from left to right) Peter Urban, Thomas LaPuppet, Joe Lewis and Chuck Norris.

Vol. 6, No. 6, 50 cents

▶ A Japanese expat in California weighs in on the actions of Americans who come to his native nation: "Every time they go to a foreign country, they end up stealing the girls."

▶ The big news in the martial arts community continues to be the upcoming *Black Belt* Hall of Fame banquet, trade show and convention. Still months off, half the exhibitor space has been reserved, and interest among instructors (students not allowed) is skyrocketing.

▶ Chuck Norris tastes defeat at Aaron Banks' First Annual East Coast vs. West Coast Championship Tournament. The man who vanquished him? Louis Delgado, who later lost to Joe Lewis.

▶ Andy Adams, *Black Belt's* Japan correspondent, reports on the intense training of the emperor's bodyguards. It spans judo, *kendo,* karate, *kyudo* and modern weapons.

▶ The editor of *Black Belt* laments that "an alarming number of *dojo* have been closing up" because of insufficient cash flow. The much-criticized commercialization of the martial arts, he says, may not be such a bad thing.

▶ Frank Smith bests Kenneth Funakoshi to win the All-America Karate Tournament in Los Angeles.

▶ Jhoon Rhee hits it big in Washington, D.C. Five years ago, the *taekwondo* master had to borrow $400 to build a school, and now he runs five studios and boasts 1,500 students.

▶ When asked for his opinion of *Black Belt's* International Convention of the Martial Arts, Bruce Lee is enthusiastic but expresses some reservations about the skill level of some of the people he fears will attend: "You'll get a lot of phonies, guys who want to come to a convention to say that they came to a convention. I think there are more phonies in the art of *gung fu* today than in any other art."

▶ An Italian rag—I mean, mag—named *Cintura Nera* blatantly steals *Black Belt's* text and photos. Los Angeles-based publisher M. Uyehara reads them the riot act and threatens legal action if they don't cease and desist.

▶ *Black Belt* Hall of Fame member Ki Whang Kim organizes an eight-day multiart summer camp in West Virginia. The tuition is a reasonable $75.

▶ Joe Corley, the martial artist who would later found the Battle of Atlanta, places first in the black-belt division at the 1968 Metro Atlanta Team and Individual Championship Tournament.

▶ When a reader writes in to scold *Black Belt* for its dearth of coverage of the then-rare-in-America art of *jujutsu,* the editor replies: "If you admit that jujutsu is overlooked and needs revival, then you have to admit that the magazine must, by necessity, focus on the more popular martial arts. We report the field, not make the field."

WORLD'S LEADING MAGAZINE OF SELF-DEFENSE   JULY 1968 ⊠ 50 CENTS

BLACK BELT

SPECIAL REPORT:

WOMEN IN SELF-DEFENSE!

THE MASK OF SILAT: The bloody sport of the Philippines!

JUJITSU's EMPTY LEGACY: Last stand for an idealist.

ISSUE FIFTY-FIVE | JULY 1968

The 55th issue of *Black Belt* was dated July 1968. It was 66 pages long and featured Kathy Phillips on the cover.

Vol. 6, No. 7, 50 cents

▶ *Black Belt* founder M. Uyehara argues that protective gear will soon become the key to ensuring the safety of competitors and ending the days when "the out-of-control practitioner is king."

▶ The going rate for karate lessons: $15 a month if you go four times a week.

▶ The *Black Belt*-sponsored International Convention of the Martial Arts is stirring up controversy, and it's still three months away. It seems that a number of instructors across the country are up in arms because one discussion topic will be race relations in the *dojo*. In related news, Mas Oyama agrees to speak at the event.

▶ Japanese educators fear that their nation's improving lifestyle is making kids soft. Many are pinning their hopes for hardening up the next generation on judo, karate, *aikido* and *kendo* training.

▶ In his profile of *jujutsu* master Toichiro Takeuchi, Japan correspondent Andy Adams writes: "Strange as it seems, hitting a man when he's down is an important part of jujutsu. Kicking, too. Once the throw is completed, the thrower usually follows through with a sharp kick—to the temple or between the eyes."

▶ Need an ashtray with a gold-plated side-kicking figurine in the middle? It'll set you back $7.90.

▶ To generate its cover story, *Black Belt* hosts a round-table discussion on the blossoming number of women in the martial arts. When the managing editor asks the panel if ladies are signing up just to meet men, Kathy Phillips insists, "Karate isn't a man-chasing sport."

▶ The magazine sends a reporter to the Philippines to investigate *silat,* which was reportedly imported from other Southeast Asian nations. After incessantly nagging his government hosts, the intrepid writer is able to bypass the watered-down tourist shows and experience the true art of war in remote tribal areas.

▶ More than 100 karate clubs are operating in England, 30 of which are in London.

▶ A New England-based competitor laments the venue conditions during a recent event: "Grease and dirt [on the floors] put the Korean stylists at a disadvantage as we could not execute many of the techniques without fear of injury."

▶ A reader from Stockton, California, implores *Black Belt* readers to preserve their back issues. "I have two copies of the first issue ... in excellent condition," he writes. "They are for sale for $100 each or trade for something of equal value." Fast-forward to 2004: It's been reported that pint-size copies of that monumental magazine sell for as much as $400.

WORLD'S LEADING MAGAZINE OF SELF-DEFENSE

AUGUST 1968 50 CENTS

BLACK BELT

CLOSEUP: THOMAS LA PUPPET

this east coast karate
warhorse continues to thrill
tournament players, spectators

THE BARNUM OF BRAWL

Dressed Up In Showbiz Garb,
Tai Chi Chuan Is Still An
Effective Self-Defense Weapon

LAST
CALL!

icma

ISSUE FIFTY-SIX | AUGUST 1968

The 56th issue of *Black Belt* was dated August 1968. It was 66 pages long and featured a black-and-white photo of Thomas LaPuppet on the cover.

Vol. 6, No. 8, 50 cents

▶ When an impatient reader expresses his doubts that Bruce Lee will ever finish composing *Tao of Jeet Kune Do,* the editor of *Black Belt* reassures him that Lee is hard at work putting on the finishing touches.

▶ Need martial arts medals to pass out at your next tournament? They'll set you back 55 cents apiece. Full-size trophies go for $1.40 each.

▶ For the second time, the U.S. Army declares sumo champ Jesse Kuhaulua, who wrestles in Japan as Takamiyama, too fat to fight. He thus avoids the draft.

▶ At S. Henry Cho's All-American Open Karate Championship, the 28-year-old Chuck Norris wins the grand championship. Ron Marchini and Mitchell Bobrow place first and second, respectively, at the Tournament of Champions, which is held concurrently.

▶ Thomas LaPuppet is profiled in the issue's cover story. Called the top fighter on the East Coast, he would be inducted into the *Black Belt* Hall of Fame in 1969 and pass away 30 years later.

▶ At the First Invitational Karate Tournament in Burbank, California, Bob Wall places second in the brown-belt division.

▶ Controversy erupts as William Chen claims to use the teachings of *tai chi chuan* to harden his body while slabs of rock are sledgehammered on his abdomen.

▶ A movie producer spots a *Black Belt* story about the martial arts training of the Chinese tongs (secret societies) and draws up plans to make a film.

▶ Yugoslavian *judoka* Dan Stanko Topocnik enters the First International Sambo Tournament in Latvia. After reviewing the rules the morning of the event, he places a very respectable second.

▶ Malaysian *kuntao* expert Tan Kim See is accosted by six men, four of whom are carrying spears. The martial artist survives the impaling of his arm, then KOs four of the thugs with kuntao strikes and another with a judo throw. The sixth flees.

▶ The staff of *Black Belt* is hard at work prepping for the launch of its International Convention of the Martial Arts, a show to be composed of seminars, round-table discussions, demonstrations and the like. Flash-forward to 2004, when the current staff of your favorite magazine is drawing up plans for a supersize version of the event. Projected to have four components—a film festival, a trade show, a Hall of Fame banquet and reunion, and a series of seminars—it's guaranteed to be the must-do martial arts show of 2005.

WORLD'S LEADING MAGAZINE OF SELF-DEFENSE SEPTEMBER 1968 50 CENTS

BLACK BELT

JUDO INTERNATIONAL/KARATE INTERNATIONAL TOURNAMENTS

THE GUNG-FU VIGILANTES . . . TOUGHENING KARATE FISTS

ISSUE FIFTY-SEVEN | SEPTEMBER 1968

The 57th issue of *Black Belt* was dated September 1968. It was 66 pages long and featured a color photo of Tonny Tulleners on the cover.

Vol. 6, No. 9, 50 cents

▶ As Bruce Lee grows his roster of Hollywood celebs eager to sign up for lessons, his tuition rate climbs to $500 for 10 classes.

▶ A reader in Orlando, Florida, complains about the difficulties he faces in trying to find *Black Belt* on the newsstand. The best solution then is the same as it is now: subscribe.

▶ Some things never change: *Black Belt* founder M. Uyehara pens his editorial about the rising numbers of school owners who try to get new students to commit to a six-month or longer contract. Not good for the arts, he concludes.

▶ The Sacramento (California) Judo Club stars in a series of 79 10-minute lessons produced by a local TV station. It's being made available to martial artists around the nation.

▶ The Philippines prepares to enact a law that will prohibit all ex-cons from studying or teaching the martial arts.

▶ A panel of experts discusses the value of learning the martial arts from books and magazines. Hayward Nishioka concludes that the printed word is fine for classifying techniques, but to get good, you've got to hit the mats.

▶ Australia issues a plea to the martial arts world: Send us more karate *sensei,* especially to Sydney, Perth and Melbourne.

▶ In response to the blossoming number of people taking up the martial arts in Puerto Rico, the city of San Juan is planning to construct a $40,000 *dojo*.

▶ Future *Black Belt* Hall of Fame member Takayuki Kubota weighs in on the practice of conditioning the hands on *makiwara* boards. In case you're wondering, he's in favor.

▶ *Black Belt's* book-review editor, Dr. Philip J. Rasch, picks his faves: For judo, it's *Dynamic Judo: Throwing Techniques* and *Dynamic Judo: Grappling Techniques* by Kazuzo Kudo; for karate, it's *Art of Empty Hand Fighting* by Hidetaka Nishiyama and Richard C. Brown; for *aikido,* it's *The Arts of Self-Defense* by Koichi Tohei; and for miscellaneous arts, it's *Secrets of Chinese Leg Maneuvers* by Lee Ying-Arng.

▶ Burt Ward, the actor who portrays Robin in the *Batman* TV series, gets his purple belt in karate.

▶ Aaron Banks hatches a plan that would eliminate most of the "inconsequential" karate tournaments in favor of one huge one in New York City.

▶ After losing a bout to Luis Delgado and another to Joe Lewis, Chuck Norris waxes philosophical in an article titled "The Practical Art of Losing." He says, "When you lose, no matter what, it's better to lose to a gracious and polite winner. It hurts less."

WORLD'S LEADING MAGAZINE OF SELF-DEFENSE   OCTOBER 1968   50 CENTS

BLACK BELT

▶ **PRO KARATE CHAMPIONSHIPS — THE INSIDE STORY!**

▶ **THE REVOLT OF THE SUMOS! NOW IT CAN BE TOLD!**

Naginata! An in-depth view of this dynamic martial art where women are kings!

ISSUE FIFTY-EIGHT | OCTOBER 1968

The 58th issue of *Black Belt* was dated October 1968. It was 66 pages long and featured a color photo of a *kendoka* and a *naginata* practitioner on the cover.

Vol. 6, No. 10, 50 cents

▶ After watching an exhibition of Thai-style kickboxing, some Tokyo martial artists insist it's nothing but "lethargic karate."

▶ Bruce Lee scores work as the consultant for an upcoming Dean Martin movie. He immediately starts contacting the top names in the karate world to play the heroes and villains.

▶ Five Brazilian *capoeira* masters join forces to deliver a plea to the United States: Help us spread our once-outlawed art across America. It's assumed that the local practice of taping razor blades to the practitioners' feet will not be transported to stateside schools.

▶ *Black Belt* founder M. Uyehara opines that Aaron Banks' proposed remedy for the plunging popularity of karate tournaments—the creation of a pro circuit—may work, but a simpler solution exists: Event directors merely need to work together to further the sport.

▶ After losing a match to Paul Pelela nearly a year ago, Joe Lewis unleashes a hot and heavy onslaught that decimates his foe at the First Annual Tournament of Champions in Seattle. Karate's "bad boy" goes on to take the grand-championship title.

▶ Need headgear for your *kendo* or naginata class? You can nab one for $40.

▶ Japan's Ministry of Education lists only eight licensed naginata instructors in the nation's school system. Across the country, some 10,000 nonstudents (read: adults) study the art.

▶ Ed Parker holds the Hawaii-U.S. Mainland Competition, and some of the top names in the karate world strut their stuff. Thomas LaPuppet wins his matches, then announces his retirement. Newcomer Ron Marchini proves he's one to watch in the competitive world. Mike Stone lives up to his reputation with three victories, as does Tonny Tulleners. Skipper Mullins, Allen Steen and Arnold Urquidez don't fare as well. Dave Krieger surprises everyone with his victory over Chuck Norris, forcing the champ to walk away with two victories and one loss.

▶ Andy Adams, *Black Belt's* Japan correspondent, lands a broadcasting job with the CBS TV network.

▶ A novel idea for a competition is spawned in Tacoma, Washington: Instead of using referees, the martial artists in the sparring division call the points themselves. Surprisingly, few arguments ensue.

▶ An American in Japan writes in to lodge what will become a familiar gripe: "One thing about these famous *dojo* is that you may train and train and never see the great man you're studying under. Even [Mas] Oyama only trains his black belts twice a week."

WORLD'S LEADING MAGAZINE OF SELF-DEFENSE · NOVEMBER 1968 · 50 CENTS

BLACK BELT

▶ **THE BLACK BELT HALL OF FAME AWARDS 1968**

▶ **a quick course in karate · the call of aikido**

Budo Demolition: The famed Tiger Division
of the Korean Army in action!

The 59th issue of *Black Belt* was dated November 1968. It was 66 pages long and featured a color photo of soldiers from South Korea's Tiger Division on the cover.

Vol. 6, No. 11, 50 cents

▶ *Black Belt* announces the winners of its first Hall of Fame vote. In case you're wondering, they're Frank Fullerton (Man of the Year), Kiro Nagano (Judo Instructor of the Year), Tsutomu Ohshima (Karate Instructor of the Year), Hayward Nishioka (Judo Player of the Year), Chuck Norris (Karate Player of the Year), Shuji Mikami (Kendo Instructor of the Year), Koichi Tohei (Aikido Instructor of the Year) and the Detroit Judo Club (Dojo of the Year).

▶ A reader takes Chuck Norris to task over his statement that he tries techniques in competition before he's perfected them, then lambastes *Black Belt* for condoning the activity. One wonders just how many techniques would be thrown in tournaments if only "perfected" kicks and punches could be used.

▶ South Korea's Tiger Division boasts more than 200 *taekwondo* black belts who train in excess of 15,000 Korean, Vietnamese and American soldiers in Vietnam. "It is important that the troops be able to turn their techniques into devastating, bone-crushing blows," Capt. Yoon Dong-ho says. "There is no place for mild strikes in combat."

▶ An irate reader from Huntington Beach, California, tears into the Pan-American Karate Championship because he observed eight knockdowns that had to be followed by lengthy recovery periods, all in the space of two hours. He writes, "I shouldn't have to pay $5 to injure or possibly kill someone when I can do exactly the same thing on the street—for free."

▶ More than 300 citizens of Hong Kong are now practicing *aikido*. The best-known instructor is expat New Yorker Virginia Mayhew.

▶ The five-day International Convention of the Martial Arts is a big hit in Los Angeles. Hosted by *Black Belt,* it features presentations by Chuck Norris, Richard Kim, Jhoon Rhee, Hayward Nishioka and Aaron Banks.

▶ Burt Ward, who portrays Robin on the *Batman* TV series, reveals that he was forced to learn the martial arts for his role as a superhero. The "encouragement" came after a public-relations exaggeration boasted of the actor's nonexistent black belt, which caused Bruce Lee to request a sparring session with him. Wisely, Ward declined.

▶ In a series of United States-South Korea grudge matches held under the innocuous title of International Championships, Joe Lewis faces Ju-hum Kim. Angry at his opponent's attempt to call a timeout instead of fighting it out, Lewis grabs Kim and chucks him to the mat. That prompts the Korean team to pile on the lone American. "One of the Koreans unleashed a fierce kick while another hammered his face," a reporter wrote. "Lewis shot out some punches, which connected hard and fast and was finally restrained by the referee."

▶ Then it's Ron Marchini's turn. The same Korean calls a timeout and exits the ring, prompting Marchini to follow and toss him to the floor for some ground-and-pound. After they're separated, Kim blasts Marchini with a face punch that busts his beak. The American slams his foe down and jumps on top, but the ref pulls them apart. Kim offers Marchini his hand in friendship, and as the American walks forward to accept, Kim clocks him with a roundhouse to the head. All in a day's work.

WORLD'S LEADING MAGAZINE OF SELF-DEFENSE

DECEMBER 1968 50 CENTS

BLACK BELT

KARATE'S KANGAROO COURT: ORIENT vs. U.S.

THE CAT OF KUNG-FU • SEINO'S CHAMPIONSHIP JUDO

Kick boxing versus karate. Which one is superior? Karatemen call it devastating!

ISSUE SIXTY | DECEMBER 1968

The 60ᵗʰ issue of *Black Belt* was dated December 1968. It was 66 pages long and featured a black-and-white photo of two kickboxers on the cover.

Vol. 6, No. 12, 50 cents

▶ Fumio Demura stars in six 20-minute film reels dedicated to the *sai.* The set will set you back $60. If you'd also like a pair of sai designed by the master, they will cost you $23.95.

▶ A reader from Virginia who attended *Black Belt's* first International Convention of the Martial Arts writes to thank Bruce Lee for taking the time out of his hectic schedule to visit with his child and offer some encouraging words for the aspiring martial artist.

▶ Two Japanese *judoka* breach the Iron Curtain to demonstrate the grappling art in Hungary, Bulgaria, Yugoslavia and Czechoslovakia.

▶ *Black Belt* announces the impending publication of its first yearbook. It will cost 75 cents if you're a subscriber and $1 if you aren't.

▶ A *karateka* from Massachusetts complains about the conduct he observed at the recent tournament: "There was pushing, clawing, kicking, unsportsmanlike gestures and hard contact. Where was the technique, the form, the control?" It seems that some things never change.

▶ After teaching at Osan Air Base in South Korea for six years, *hapkido* legend Bong Soo Han relocates to the United States.

▶ *Black Belt* examines the new sport of kickboxing, which is all the rage in Japan. "The following tactics are forbidden: thumbing the eyes, biting, attacking the groin, hitting a downed opponent, choking, and twisting the arms and legs." All else is fair game, including attacking from the front, side or rear; chopping with the hands; elbow strikes; head butts; and throws.

▶ Item for the look-how-far-we've-come department: African-American martial artist Hulon Willis pens an exposé on prejudice in the *dojo,* and Aaron Banks' Orient vs. the U.S. tournament is described as a "racist purge against the Asians."

▶ France is now home to 311 karate black belts, at least according to the records of the nation's official karate association.

▶ It's only in an age of innocence—or ignorance—that one can imagine the publication of a book titled *Kung Fu* by an author identified as The Honorable Master "Kung Fu." *Black Belt* gives it a thumbs down.

WORLD'S LEADING MAGAZINE OF SELF-DEFENSE   JANUARY 1969   50 CENTS

BLACK BELT

TOMIKI: MAVERICK OF THE MARTIAL ARTS
THE DREAM MATCH THAT BECAME A NIGHTMARE

KARATE FREE-SPARRING FOR BEGINNERS
Tatsuo Suzuki points out some
facets in karate which the
beginners may overlook!

ISSUE SIXTY-ONE | JANUARY 1969

The 61st issue of *Black Belt* was dated January 1969. It was 66 pages long and featured a color photo of Tatsuo Suzuki on the cover.

Vol. 7, No. 1, 50 cents

▶ Chuck Norris officially retires after Ki Whang Kim's Third American Invitational Karate Championships.

▶ A vacationing California resident marvels at finding *Black Belt* in a martial arts school in Formosa—that's Taiwan for all you youngsters.

▶ Sigoyo Kuniba, president of the Seishin Kai International Martial Arts Federation of Tokyo, visits the United States.

▶ While bemoaning the lack of discipline in homes and schools, M. Uyehara, founder and editor of *Black Belt,* announces that America's *dojo* have stepped up to the plate and begun teaching decency, sportsmanship and character development.

▶ A Singapore martial artist claims he earned his third-degree black belt from Mas Oyama after defeating 100 men in combat. Naysayers insist he battled only 20 and failed to best all of them.

▶ An international incident nearly erupts in the Philippines when a high-ranked Japanese judo master snubs *Black Belt's* correspondent. Fortunately, the newly created doctrine of mutually assured destruction, or MAD, keeps the nukes in their silos.

▶ The National Polytechnic Institute in Mexico City adds judo to its course offerings.

▶ A writer is shocked when instructor George Cofield admits that he's told his karate students it's OK to strike with full force in tournaments.

▶ The trendy lines of the judo *gi* are a hit in Paris' fashion circles.

▶ *Black Belt* introduces *iaido,* the art of drawing the sword, to the American public. In Japan, students of the style fork over $1 to $1.50 a month for tuition. Among their first lessons is a little gem that says the resistance encountered as a *katana* blade slices through a two-year-old bamboo stalk approximates what's needed to bisect a man's leg.

▶ Seventeen-year-old Mitchell Bobrow triumphs over Joe Lewis in overtime at the Tae Gyun Championship Tournament in Philadelphia.

▶ Having honed a few throws and won a few competitions shouldn't lead to excessive pride, says ninth-degree black-belt Kazuo Ito, for a judo champion is not necessarily a judo master.

▶ When a reader's wife takes up judo, the happy hubby posts a letter to *Black Belt:* "In the beginning, it was a joke to see her attempts at throwing me. Now I find it difficult, and at times impossible, to prevent her from throwing me. Not only do I respect her for this, but I also find her immensely more appealing."

WORLD'S LEADING MAGAZINE OF SELF-DEFENSE
FEBRUARY 1969 ⬥ 50 CENTS

BLACK BELT

▸ YOU ARE A LETHAL WEAPON! — SO SAYS THE LAW!

▸ THE INNER BATTLE OF KARATE'S FIGHTING LEATHERNECK

Pain! Accidents in judo, karate. How to lessen pain revealed.

ISSUE SIXTY-TWO | FEBRUARY 1969

The 62nd issue of *Black Belt* was dated February 1969. It was 66 pages long and featured a color photo of two battling *karateka* on the cover.

Vol. 7, No. 2, 50 cents

▶ On-screen, Bruce Lee threatens James Garner's character in MGM's *Little Sister* and tutors Dean Martin for Columbia Pictures' *The Wrecking Crew.* Assisting Lee in the latter film are Chuck Norris, Joe Lewis, Ed Parker, Mike Stone and Bill Ryusaki.

▶ As more and more martial artists jump on the bash-all-tournaments bandwagon, a reader from Rhode Island congratulates Hidy Ochiai, organizer of a competition in Binghamton, New York, for a job well done.

▶ Frank Fullerton, the first Man of the Year in the *Black Belt* Hall of Fame, lauds the magazine for organizing the International Convention of the Martial Arts. His wish for it to become an annual event may not have come true, but on July 29, 30 and 31, 2005, a bigger and better show hosted by *Black Belt* will outshine it by several magnitudes.

▶ *Black Belt* editor M. Uyehara takes a potshot at Hidetaka Nishiyama's Invitational World Karate Championship. It was "one of the most dull tournaments to have ever graced the karate scene," he writes.

▶ Recently elected director of the Japan Karate Association in the United States, Fumio Demura is tasked with uniting all karate practitioners in America. Good luck.

▶ Trying to mimic the winning 1966 performance of John Ryan, a *judoka* who clandestinely entered the Cornish Wrestling Championship in England and won, three British judo practitioners fare well but ultimately fall short.

▶ Honolulu-based Patrick Hodges defends the honor of kung fu, which was attacked in a recent cartoon comparing it to *jeet kune do:* "The sets of classical kung fu are not meant to be used in real combat situations but serve as a sort of dictionary from which one chooses his favorite techniques."

▶ The state of the art in protective gear arrives. It consists of a vest- or jacket-style torso shield, shinguards and arm guards, a *kendo* head cage and a "crotch guard." The whole kit and caboodle will set you back $97.

▶ In an article introducing *Black Belt* readers to the fighting systems of India and Pakistan, it's revealed that both nations have forbidden the manufacture of most traditional martial arts weapons.

▶ Following a storm of controversy over his match with Chuck Norris, as reported in the December 1968 issue of *Black Belt,* Skipper Mullins writes: "I wanted to win the championship so bad it hurt, and I wanted to take it from one of the best, Mr. Chuck Norris, but he was a little sharper that night and came back and beat me." Humility is refreshing, isn't it?

WORLD'S LEADING MAGAZINE OF SELF-DEFENSE

MARCH 1969 50 CENTS

BLACK BELT

▶ THE SLINGSHOT ARSENAL OF JUDO'S ISAO OKANO

▶ TRUE! THE PURGE OF THE PELL STREET TONGS

THE NUNCHAKU: Terror For Human Targets! The powerful weapon at work!

ISSUE SIXTY-THREE | MARCH 1969

The 63rd issue of *Black Belt* was dated March 1969. It was 66 pages long and featured a color photo of Fumio Demura on the cover.

Vol. 7, No. 3, 50 cents

▶ On the subject of karate going pro, publisher M. Uyehara writes: "The supporters of professional *budo* compare the trend with professional golf, but why not with professional wrestling or, for that matter, the roller derby?"

▶ Karate in Brazil is overseen by the Brazilian Confederation of Pugilism. Catchy name, isn't it?

▶ Philadelphia-based Mohn Suh Park educates the Western world about *tae kyon,* a rare Korean kicking art that's believed to have influenced the development of *taekwondo.*

▶ Future *Black Belt* Hall of Fame member Peter Urban speaks out on the subject of fair judging at tournaments: "When a true corps of referees is developed in America and when their reputations are at stake, then and only then will all the partiality and lying come to a stop."

▶ In the cover story, Fumio Demura teaches the *nunchaku,* the Okinawan weapon that has mesmerized America. Because they're so hard to come by, most practitioners have been making their own.

▶ Controversy erupts at the U.S. Karate Championship when the nine women who entered subsequently withdraw. Organizer Gary Alexander reportedly refused to set up a female division and told them they would have to compete against the men.

▶ Mike Stone demos a new training dummy he designed. He claims it hones a student's kicks and punches while promoting accuracy and power.

▶ In a scathing review of a tournament held under the auspices of the All-America Karate Federation, Thomas Dugan writes: "In the early '60s, the *shotokan* system was one of the strongest organizations on the American scene. It appears that satisfaction has led to stagnation. … In the contest, only the front kick and reverse punch were used, and both ineffectively. Many times the combatants stood toe-to-toe, exchanging weak punches. Defensive ability was almost nonexistent."

▶ A one-year subscription to *Black Belt* costs $5.75.

▶ The University of Tokyo opens a special clinic for sumo wrestlers who overeat. Apparently, it's easy to do when you consume in excess of 5,000 calories a day.

WORLD'S LEADING MAGAZINE OF SELF-DEFENSE — APRIL 1969 — 50 CENTS

BLACK BELT

THE TRIAL OF COUNT DANTE/WHAT'S <u>YOUR</u> VERDICT?

EXCLUSIVE: The Killer Art of The Headhunters!

WHAT'S A POINT? NINE KARATE REFEREES TELL YOU!

ISSUE SIXTY-FOUR | APRIL 1969

The 64th issue of *Black Belt* was dated April 1969. It was 66 pages long and featured a color photo of two tribesmen from Borneo on the cover.

Vol. 7, No. 4, 50 cents

▶ Chuck Norris, Mike Stone and Skipper Mullins plan a trip to Hawaii to call out the island's best karate fighters.

▶ Are the martial arts being watered down? A man from Lincoln, Illinois, claims his *sensei* won't teach anything dangerous to his students until they attain the rank of first-degree black belt.

▶ A man destined to become quite well-known in the martial arts community writes in to ream *Black Belt* for its often-negative book reviews. His name is Willem de Thouars.

▶ A medical doctor weighs in on the realities of *katsu* (or *kappo),* the Japanese art of resuscitation: "The unskilled application of the techniques not only is ineffective but also may be dangerous. Experimentation may result in serious injury or even loss of life."

▶ After Bill Wallace bests Joe Hayes and Steve Sanders at Aaron Banks' annual New York karate competition, he's hailed as the best fighter of the tournament and a man with the class of a champion.

▶ The controversial Count Dante, aka John Keehan, is profiled in an eight-page feature.

▶ Tatsuo Suzuki teams up with Hironori Ohtsuka to establish the Wado-Kai Section of the All-Japan Karate-Do Federation in London.

▶ *Kuntau bangkui,* the war art of the headhunters of central Borneo, is introduced to American martial artists. For some reason, it never caught on.

▶ In a revealing discourse on the subjective nature of officiating, a cadre of renowned referees gives reasons why certain techniques fail to score: "The attacker did not keep watching the opponent," "The [kicker's] heel was off the floor," "The attacker had a weak stance," and "The upper part of the body was leaning too far backward to generate any power."

▶ Hayward Nishioka demonstrates judo isotonics—specifically, using trees and parked cars to provide resistance for throwing drills.

▶ A 55-year-old woman uses her karate skills to foil two would-be purse snatchers. She reportedly struck the first man in the abdomen and throat and the second in the throat and "elsewhere."

▶ California-based Fumio Demura accomplishes a similar feat, but with only one crime-breaking thug to deal with, he barely breaks a sweat.

WORLD'S LEADING MAGAZINE OF SELF-DEFENSE

MAY 1969 50 CENTS

BLACK BELT

PRO/KARATE:
NORTH and
SOUTH

PULLING
KARATE
PUNCHES
What's The Point?

THE POWER-PLAY
OF ANTON GEESINK

ISSUE SIXTY-FIVE | MAY 1969

The 65th issue of *Black Belt* was dated May 1969. It was 66 pages long and featured a color photo of a fist on the cover.

Vol. 7, No. 5, 50 cents

▶ The staff of *Black Belt* lays the foundation for its Second International Convention of the Martial Arts, to take place in New York City. Fast-forward to 2005, when the current staff is putting the finishing touches on plans for *Black Belt's* 1st Annual Festival of Martial Arts, on tap for July 29-31 at Universal Studios Hollywood.

▶ A karate practitioner in Chicago thwarts an attempt at grand-theft auto by flashing his *shodan* ID card.

▶ In tournament commentary following the First Professional Karate Championship, Warren C. Walitzer writes: "After Luis Delgado had lost a hard match to Chuck Norris and Mike Stone was fighting Bob Taianni, Bob tore the sleeve off Mike's *gi*. As Mike pulled off his jacket in disgust, Delgado generously pulled off his own jacket and threw it to Mike. Stone threw it back, saying, 'I go with the winners.' Then he accepted Chuck's jacket."

▶ Want some cheap protective gear? You can pick up a full-body set of Karate Econo-Tectors for a tad more than $30.

▶ A member of the U.S. Special Forces based in Japan reveals the true lethality of karate: "Okinawans and Japanese wear pointed shoes. A partial block of a front kick results in at least a broken hand, and if it gets through, you are 'toes up.' "

▶ In his editorial, the managing editor of *Black Belt* nails down one reason the mag has always been the industry leader: "Unlike many publications, we are consciously involved with the goings-on in the martial arts. We intend to remain this way."

▶ A martial artist from Brooklyn, New York, sets the record straight: The famed edged weapon of India isn't called a *gurka* or *gurkha*. Its proper name is *kukri*.

▶ When *Black Belt* hosts a forum on the pros and cons of pulling punches in the *dojo*, S. Henry Cho weighs in: "We do our best to avoid injuries, but the students must expect some injuries in free fighting. Some people come to us and think they will become karate players by meditating and thinking about it."

▶ A journalist reports that more than 300,000 Japanese swords are in the United States, many of them brought back by servicemen returning after the occupation.

▶ In an early nod to the silliness of many knife-defense techniques, Dr. Philip J. Rasch writes in his review of a self-defense book, "Instructions to catch the blow in midair cause [me] to turn pale."

▶ An enterprising reader from Kansas seems blissfully unaware of a potential investment. He writes, "For those interested in the first volume of *Black Belt,* I have a copy in mint condition and will sell it to the highest bidder." If he'd kept it for the next four decades, it'd be worth more than 800 times what he paid.

WORLD'S LEADING MAGAZINE OF SELF-DEFENSE

JUNE 1969 50 CENTS

BLACK BELT

THE BATTLING
MONKS OF CHI-CHI

TOOLS FOR
KARATE TRAINING

THE BLACK POWER OF CAPOEIRA

ISSUE SIXTY-SIX | JUNE 1969

The 66th issue of *Black Belt* was dated June 1969. It was 66 pages long and featured a color photo of two *capoeira* practitioners on the cover.

Vol. 7, No. 6, 50 cents

► A reader from the Bronx, New York, pleads for help from *Black Belt* to get *The Green Hornet* back on television. "They should have disposed of *Batman* because this TV show was stupid," he writes. "Two grown men running around in tights!"

► *Black Belt* launches *Karate Illustrated,* a new publication dedicated to covering the expanding tournament scene.

► As the magazine organizes the second installment of its International Convention of the Martial Arts, more than 1,000 practitioners are expected to attend from host city New York. Among the festivities will be the *Black Belt* Hall of Fame Awards Banquet.

► A Japanese survey reveals that 29 percent of Tokyo "pushers"—people whose job it is to shove passengers into subway cars—have studied karate, judo or football.

► Chuck Norris, Joe Lewis and Fumio Demura are slated to attend the convention, but Gene LeBell has to bow out because of a movie commitment. Fast-forward to 2005: Those four masters, along with more than 30 others, have promised to attend the *Black Belt* festival, scheduled for July 29-31 at Universal Studios Hollywood.

► S. Henry Cho generates controversy when he threatens to expose all the so-called Korean champions who've opened schools in the United States.

► Mitchell Bobrow bags the grand championship at the All-American Karate Tournament in New York City.

► In a story about capoeira, it's claimed that the Brazilian government officially acknowledged the African martial art only after it was watered down into a cultural dance.

► A landmark study concludes that exposure to karate techniques—specifically, the side, forward and reverse punch—via home movies really can improve a person's technique.

► In a piece on his fighting philosophy, Korean-American martial arts legend Richard Kim states: "Karate begins where *kempo* ends. Both teach self-defense, but kempo, as practiced in America, relies on technical efficiency. Karate goes beyond physical excellence and strives for spiritual attainment."

► Rebutting a kung fu practitioner who sang the praises of his art's sets as the perfect preparation for fighting, Joe Lewis puts pen to paper. "For psychological development of combat skills, one needs an opponent, not a cooperative partner," he writes. "Many paths will lead to the mountain, but the wrong path will lead nowhere."

► At the First International Open Karate Championships, women's-division referee Ed Kaloudis is forced to "put a stranglehold on one of the girls to keep her from killing her opponent."

WORLD'S LEADING MAGAZINE OF SELF-DEFENSE

JULY 1969 50 CENTS

BLACK BELT

THE TONFA—SPINNING FURY

MAULERS OF MONGOLIA

THE DEATH CRY OF GI-TODAN

ISSUE SIXTY-SEVEN | JULY 1969

The 67th issue of *Black Belt* was dated July 1969. It was 66 pages long and featured a color photo of Okinawan master Jun Kina on the cover.

Vol. 7, No. 7, 50 cents

▶ Nine foreigners make headlines in Korea when they test for black belt alongside some 200 locals.

▶ A member of the Montgomery Police Department in Alabama commends *Black Belt* on its coverage of traditional weaponry: "The *[nunchaku]* is much more practical in this day and age than the *sai.*" Hmm ... must be a rough town.

▶ A *kendo* team is so irked when producers of *The Tonight Show Starring Johnny Carson* postpone its appearance two nights in a row that on the third night, the martial artists bolt, leaving the studio execs high and dry.

▶ A reader from Calgary, Canada, voices a valid point: Students often drop out of martial arts schools because they're forced to develop all their techniques equally. No one is ever "allowed" to skip *kata,* for example. "Not everyone on a baseball team can be the pitcher," he claims, "but they can all be ballplayers."

▶ Despite the war, more than 100 martial artists gather in Phan Dinh Pung for the 1968 Vietnam Taekwondo Championships.

▶ While traveling in the Soviet Union, an American who's living in Japan secures permission to visit Mongolia. The result? A wrestling article titled "The Maulers of Mongolia," featuring the spiritual progeny of Genghis Khan.

▶ The coolest financial institution in Quezon City, Philippines, is a bank branch staffed solely by women. "Behind their cages," Antonio V. Mendoza writes, "these women have ... know-how in the fighting skills of *aikido,* karate and judo."

▶ Controversy rages over a recent story about Count Dante, aka John Keehan, prompting *Black Belt's* D. David Dreis to ask, "Is Keehan guilty or innocent of blasphemy to the martial arts?"

▶ *Tonfa* training is great for self-defense, it's claimed, but its real value lies in the way it works the body. "A *karateka* without much agility cannot concentrate on the weapon if he must concentrate on his body."

▶ At the United States Invitational Karate Tournament in Dallas, Fred Wren battles Jim Harrison in front of Mike Stone, Chuck Norris, Jhoon Rhee and Pat Burleson. Talk about star-studded! (Wren wins the grand championship, by the way.)

▶ When a California karateka criticizes *Black Belt's* tournament coverage as one-sided, the editor replies: "One of the biggest fallacies about journalism is that there is objective reporting. Everything you read is interpreted through the eyes of the reporter. While we at *Black Belt* try to give an honest report, an honest view, it is, of course, based on the premise that our writers are honest people."

WORLD'S LEADING MAGAZINE OF SELF-DEFENSE

AUGUST 1969   50 CENTS

BLACK BELT

PRAYING MANTIS: THE LETHAL KUNG-FU ART!

KARATE HIP POWER: DESIGNED FOR DESTRUCTION!

ISSUE SIXTY-EIGHT | AUGUST 1969

The 68th issue of *Black Belt* was dated August 1969. It was 66 pages long and featured a color photo of kung fu expert Gin Foon Mark on the cover.

Vol. 7, No. 8, 50 cents

▶ At a photo op Down Under, Japanese sumo giant Taiho poses with a 6-foot-3-inch-tall kangaroo. The marsupial, apparently not a fan of the wrestler, starts choking him with its front legs. It takes two of Taiho's teammates to subdue the beast.

▶ The Four Seasons Karate Tournament in Torrance, California, attracts 417 competitors. Produced by Chuck Norris, Bob Wall and Mike Stone, it sees a brown-belt team composed of Arnold Urquidez, Armondo Urquidez and Bill Ryusaki win top honors.

▶ In a tirade against shady instructors who reportedly accept juvenile delinquents into their *dojo,* a freedom-loving reader from New York concludes, "There should be laws about who can and can't learn karate."

▶ Presaging the reality-fighting craze of the 21st century, Richard Mendes writes: "Karate in not a beautiful art. It is a fighting art, and fighting is never beautiful."

▶ The International Judo Federation nixes South Africa's bid to join. The reason? Apartheid.

▶ At Bob Jones University in Greenville, South Carolina, a group called the Judo Gentlemen works to propagate Christianity along with the Japanese grappling sport.

▶ A military man from North Carolina is enraged at *Black Belt's* decision to cover the new art of kickboxing. "I felt like tearing up the magazine," he writes.

▶ At the Belgrade National Championships in Yugoslavia, a fighter disagrees with the referee and winds up slugging him. Problem is, the roughed-up ref is also president of the country's karate federation. He promptly bans the upstart for life.

▶ It takes a new student three-plus years to learn the physical facet of praying mantis kung fu, claims Gin Foon Mark. Next up is two years to learn the *"jujutsu*-like *dar mak* technique" that deals with vital points on the body, three years for Chinese medicine and two years for the mental side of the art. "There are few takers in today's society," he laments.

▶ The referees at a tournament sponsored by Gary Alexander reportedly wear guns because of the anarchy that erupted at a previous event.

▶ Masatoshi Nakayama of the prestigious Japan Karate Association offers sage advice on power punching: "Power generated by rotating the hips is conveyed to the backbone. After that, it goes to the muscles of the chest and shoulders, and finally to the arm and fist. The trunk works as the drive shaft."

▶ Andy Adams, *Black Belt's* Japan correspondent, lifts the veil of secrecy surrounding the nation's evil Black Dragon Society. Evidently, a bunch of *ninjutsu*-trained thugs dispatched by the espionage and assassination network succeeded at murdering the queen of Korea at the end of the 19th century.

▶ If you can't be a judo competitor, at least be a judo supporter. Seriously, judo supporters, made from "superfine two-way stretch-knit elastic," are selling for two bucks a crack.

WORLD'S LEADING MAGAZINE OF SELF-DEFENSE

SEPTEMBER 1969 50 CENTS

BLACK BELT

MAJOR SLUGFEST! THE NATIONAL KARATE TOURNEY!
CONCLUSION: JAPAN'S SINISTER BLACK DRAGON SOCIETY!

SPECIAL: Complete Coverage of the All-Japan Judo Tournament

ISSUE SIXTY-NINE | SEPTEMBER 1969

The 69th issue of *Black Belt* was dated September 1969. It was 66 pages long and featured a color photo of two battling *karateka* on the cover.

Vol. 7, No. 9, 50 cents

▶ Morihei Uyeshiba, founder of *aikido,* dies at age 86. He outlives Jigoro Kano and Gichin Funakoshi, who along with Uyeshiba, are collectively known as the Big Three.

▶ A loyal reader from England writes in to correct an article from the previous month's issue: There aren't 100 karate clubs in the United Kingdom, he says; there are 200.

▶ At a sword-defense demonstration in Washington, Akio Minakami's *katana* slips and slices his assistant's side. Onlooking Cub Scouts are shocked but not terribly traumatized by the mishap.

▶ A German judo instructor is stripped of his rank because he didn't convey the *bushido* philosophy to his students.

▶ A scene that could have been lifted straight out of a sitcom plays out in Western Australia. A man is seen kicking and screaming in the backyard of a house in Cottesloe. His frantic neighbor reports him to the police, insisting that he's acting and talking like he's James Bond. The man's verbal references to Mr. No—Dr. No was Bond's nemesis in the first 007 film—and Mr. Fleming—Ian Fleming penned the Bond novels—do nothing to substantiate his sanity. Turns out the "nut" is a martial arts student, Mr. No is his Korean instructor and Mr. Fleming is chairman of the Australia Judo Technical Board.

▶ At Riley Hawkins' *dojo* in Baltimore, students pay 50 cents a week to train.

▶ Joe Lewis defends his title at Jhoon Rhee's National Karate Tournament in Washington, D.C. Among the other competitors who fare well are Bob Wall, Jim Harrison and Riley Hawkins.

▶ When a cologne company prepares to release a new product called Black Belt, execs ask the staff of the magazine to recommend karateka who might want to appear in the commercials.

▶ Bill Wallace leads his team to victory at the Owensboro (Kentucky) Karate Championships.

▶ A 9-year-old *judoka* dies after being thrown in a match in California.

▶ The world's best-known martial arts poster— the one that shows the front and back of a man whose left arm is raised overhead to show all the vital points—goes on sale for $1.95.

▶ In his report on the 1969 East Coast Open Karate Championships, John T. McGee writes: "The only black mark on the tournament was the antagonism shown by Gary Alexander in denying a Korean *sensei* a plaque for his student's efforts. The Koreans had generally boycotted his tournament."

▶ After a female martial artist asks for more coverage of topics related to women and *Black Belt* agrees to deliver, a man from New Jersey writes, "There's nothing informative going on concerning women in the field, so please don't degrade your magazine by featuring them." Ouch!

WORLD'S LEADING MAGAZINE OF SELF-DEFENSE

OCTOBER 50 CENTS

BLACK BELT

KNUCKLE FRACTURE:
Will Your Punch
Punish You?

23 YEARS TO KILL:
The Challenge of
Chain Combat!

ISSUE SEVENTY | OCTOBER 1969

The 70th issue of *Black Belt* was dated October 1969. It was 66 pages long and featured a color photo of Pat Johnson on the cover.

Vol. 7, No. 10, 50 cents

▶ Think the mixed martial artists of the 21st century are cutting edge? Think again. In 1969 a *Black Belt* reader from San Francisco writes, "Karate should be Americanized so that a person works out as a boxer with heavy-bag striking and sparring. Too much time is spent practicing one way and performing in another."

▶ Smitten with the Korean art of *taekwondo,* more than 110,000 Vietnamese now kick and punch regularly. Many of them are earning their black belt in less than a year.

▶ Korean martial missionaries are also spreading their style in Israel and attracting attention by offering scholarships to train in the art's homeland. "Israel, like Korea, is surrounded by hostile nations," expatriate Kim Sang Jin says. "With [taekwondo], we can help in our survival."

▶ Chuck Norris prepares to launch an instructional karate series on educational television.

▶ *Black Belt's* publisher tells a tale of woe involving a hapless *aikidoka:* "An instructor from the United States went to visit the Aikido Hombu in Japan after several months of preparatory training to develop his stamina. After 15 minutes of working out with a fifth *dan* and a fourth dan, he was completely exhausted. The late founder of *aikido,* Morihei Uyeshiba, saw what was happening and reprimanded the two for tiring the newcomer."

▶ Heads-up from the *Journal of the American Medical Association:* Protect your fourth and fifth metacarpals! In nondoc talk, that means take care of your ring finger and pinkie when punching because their slim bones are most prone to breakage.

▶ Peddlers of tabloids scream "Karate Murder Case" on the streets of London, leading worrywarts to fear that the sensationalism will spell the death of the martial arts in the United Kingdom.

▶ At the Four Seasons-Spring Tournament in Torrance, California, Allen Steen's brown-belt team gets rowdy. "Contacts were so numerous that the judges and referees had to get into the act, too," *Black Belt's* reporter writes. "One official threw a contestant twice: once into the bleachers and again onto the floor after just picking him up off his feet. Both times, the contestant was hurt, and time had to be called."

▶ A half-dozen members of a public-school wrestling team enter the Southwest and Colorado Open Judo Championships in Albuquerque, New Mexico. Their decision not to prepare for the event leads to the defeat of all six.

▶ Attention reality-based self-defense instructors! You're not the first martial artists to fall in love with the word "combat." It seems Castello Combative Sports in the Big Apple has started selling Combat brand karate uniforms.

WORLD'S LEADING MAGAZINE OF SELF-DEFENSE

NOVEMBER 1969 50 CENTS

BLACK BELT

MORE TO KATA
THAN MEETS
THE EYE

THE STILETTO
ART OF
SUMATRA

ISSUE SEVENTY-ONE | NOVEMBER 1969

The 71st issue of *Black Belt* was dated November 1969. It was 66 pages long and featured a color photo of Louis Delgado on the cover.

Vol. 7, No. 11, 50 cents

▶ "I have never seen anyone like Bruce Lee," gushes tournament champ and cover boy Louis Delgado. "I have met and sparred with several karate men, but Bruce was the only one who baffled me completely."

▶ On the topic of Americanizing karate, *Black Belt* founder M. Uyehara takes a shot at the commercialization of competition: "Many sponsors charge from $5 to $7 for each player entering a tournament, and sometimes there are as many as 2,000 players. This will bring in at least $10,000 to the sponsor." In 1969, that wasn't chump change.

▶ With high hopes of unifying the Japanese striking arts, the International Karate Union is founded in London.

▶ Pat Johnson develops a reputation for being a hard-nosed referee who will permit no contact in the matches he oversees in California. Meanwhile, Pat Burleson stirs up resentment in Texas for allowing absolutely no head contact.

▶ Louisville, Kentucky, gets its first *taekwondo* school under the leadership of Seoul, Korea's Nak Yong Chung.

▶ A reader from Visalia, California, ends his letter to the editor with, "I would appreciate it if you would have more articles from the West Coast." Fast-forward to 2005, when a good portion of our mail requests more coverage of the East Coast.

▶ Got *nunchaku?* If not, you can pick up a pair made of Japanese white oak for $4.50.

▶ A reader rails against a story in a previous issue of *Black Belt* that advocated adding karate and judo to college course catalogs: "I would hate like hell to train or have my boy train under a college guide. I say 'guide' because they aren't teachers but only guide the students in the courses. In fact, college students are rioting today because of so much theory and not enough facts."

▶ Regarding *silek,* the "stiletto art of Sumatra," Wyn Sargent writes, "It's a killer. Dirty, vicious, nasty. It's a no-holds-barred type of game. Only the barbarous are eligible to play. It has one objective: to kill!" Sounds like it would be a hot topic today.

▶ At the 1969 Grand National Karate Championship, Artis Simmons takes on Bill Wallace in the semifinals—and wins. Simmons then faces Joe Lewis in the finals, but his luck runs out and Lewis triumphs 3-1.

▶ "There are too many tournaments in karate today," writes Bob Faulk of Goldsboro, North Carolina. "I think they should be limited to six a year: a U.S. championship, a U.S vs. Japan championship, a North vs. South championship, an intercollegiate championship, an East vs. West championship and one other one. It would make karate more interesting as a sport." You've got to admit that he makes some sense.

WORLD'S LEADING MAGAZINE OF SELF-DEFENSE

DECEMBER 1969 ⊠ 50 CENTS

BLACK BELT

KUSARIGAMA

THE WHIRLING CHAIN AND SLASHING BLADE

"LEARN TO FIGHT TO AVOID FIGHTING"—JACK HWANG

ISSUE SEVENTY-TWO | DECEMBER 1969

The 72nd issue of *Black Belt* was dated December 1969. It was 66 pages long and featured a color photo of two Japanese martial artists on the cover.

Vol. 7, No. 12, 50 cents

▶ *"Kata* [practice is] good only for learning the fundamentals of an art," Willem de Thouars writes. "Timing and speed are the most important matters in actual combat."

▶ Amateur Athletic Union judo champ Tad Hiraoka trains Kirk Douglas for his role as a pugilist in *There Was a Crooked Man.*

▶ Tsutomu Ohshima announces that he'll undertake the creation of the American College Karate League with high hopes that the martial artists it eventually churns out will take on their Japanese counterparts.

▶ Gogen "The Cat" Yamaguchi visits Hong Kong to spread the *goju* gospel. His Japan-based organization now boasts 3,000 students.

▶ The *Black Belt* Hall of Fame honors three men posthumously: *judoka* Ronald Berndt, judoka Daniel J. Cassel and *kendo* master Torao Mori.

▶ While discussing the old ways of teaching Japanese weaponry, 78-year-old Genkichi Kikuchi says: "A disciple was taught only one kata movement a year. It was easy for a student to get the general idea of a kata, but it took him that long to have enough opportunity to use it and develop the finer points which are not immediately apparent." Dave Lowry must be smiling.

▶ A professor in Colorado sounds off on the uphill battle his peers face in trying to spread the martial arts on campus: "Ours is unfortunately still considered an un-American sport in many universities."

▶ At the ICMA Commemorative Karate Tournament, the Chinese Kung-Fu Wu-su Association awards $1,000-plus diamond-studded belts to the champions. (That's nothing to sneeze at. Back in 1969, a new Mustang would run you only $2,700.)

▶ "To fight another is wrong, but to lose a fight with another over principles you deem honorable is worse." Words of wisdom from transplanted *taekwondo* master Jack Hwang.

▶ On the controversial topic of letting white belts compete in *kumite,* Robert Hansen of Long Island, New York, writes: "I find it amusing to see two *karateka* fight for two or three minutes with neither scoring a point even though 30 to 40 kicks and punches have been thrown. I'm certain that the reason is not tremendous blocking but an improper approach to kumite. Kumite should be looked upon as two fighters meeting in battle with the intent of delivering a death blow to a vital area with maximum force and control."

WORLD'S LEADING MAGAZINE OF SELF-DEFENSE

JANUARY 1970 · 50 CENTS

BLACK BELT

TIGER MIKE STONE'S SECRET OF WINNING

WRESTLER'S THREAT TO JUDO!

ISSUE SEVENTY-THREE | JANUARY 1970

The 73rd issue of *Black Belt* was dated January 1970. It was 66 pages long and featured a color photo of Mike Stone on the cover.

Vol. 8, No. 1, 50 cents

► On the big screen, Bruce Lee co-stars with James Garner in MGM's *Marlowe.*

► *Black Belt* announces the 1969 Hall of Fame inductees: Fumio Demura, Wally Jay, Thomas LaPuppet, Ben Campbell, Sam Allred, Masato Tamura, Yukiso Yamamoto and the Jhoon Rhee Institute of Tae Kwon Do.

► A 100-percent cotton *hakama,* medium size, costs $7.75.

► Future *Black Belt* Hall of Fame member Mike Stone reveals one of his cerebral keys to winning tournaments: "It's not the style or form I compete against because what style a man has studied is really irrelevant. It boils down to one individual being better than another."

► Army Specialist Joe Bonacci is awarded the Bronze Star after he subdues a Viet Cong officer with his bare hands during a jungle ambush. Upon returning to the United States, the first thing he does is thank his karate instructor.

► In a round-table discussion on the merits of altering *kata, Black Belt* Hall of Fame member George Dillman weighs in: "America is the only nation outside of the Orient where a determined effort is being made to create new, individually styled American kata."

► S. Henry Cho claims tournament attendance is down because of the recent cancellation of Bruce Lee's *The Green Hornet* TV series.

► A New York-based friend of a famous Japanese *kendo* master is invited to accept a posthumous award at the *Black Belt* Hall of Fame banquet, also held in the Big Apple. His curt reply: "What's in it for me?"

► The Dominican Republic holds its first karate tournament. Students from the local chapter of the Jhoon Rhee Institute clean house.

► Black belts rebel at a tournament in Salt Lake City. After learning that the organizer has arranged for fencing practitioners to officiate, they refuse to compete unless other martial artists are allowed to serve as judges and referees. The organizer reluctantly agrees.

► A reader from Washington state writes, "If karate is only for self-defense, I see no reason to practice constantly or make any effort to learn [more]. I could just carry a large club, and I doubt anyone would attack me."

► More than 200 kung fu stylists and 80,000 spectators from Southeast Asia congregate in Singapore for what's later described as a "bloodletting." They're treated to a "near-impossible melee of no-holds-barred, hard-contact, street-type fighting ... with no consideration to form or art."

WORLD'S LEADING MAGAZINE OF SELF-DEFENSE

FEBRUARY 1970 **X** 50 CENTS

BLACK BELT

BOXING or KARATE?
A FIGHTER'S DILEMMA

NINJA-GARBED AND BLOODTHIRSTY: SWORDSMAN'S REIGN OF TERROR

ISSUE SEVENTY-FOUR | FEBRUARY 1970

The 74th issue of *Black Belt* was dated February 1970. It was 66 pages long and featured a double exposure of *karateka*/kickboxer Rick Taylor on the cover.

Vol. 8, No. 2, 50 cents

▶ At Aaron Banks' annual martial arts event in the Big Apple, Rex Lee bashes his noggin through a 75-pound block of ice. Tough New Yorkers, thinking the demo is rigged, begin booing—until the human icebreaker goes into convulsions and is rushed to the hospital.

▶ The more things change, the more they stay the same: The publisher of *Black Belt* warns the public not to sign long-term *dojo* contracts.

▶ The two cheapest items advertised in the magazine this month: a medium-size referee's whistle and Kwik Splint, athletic tape designed to immobilize injured joints. Each sells for less than a buck.

▶ Despite the recent Russian invasion, judo-club membership in Czechoslovakia is on the rise.

▶ Rodger Shimatsu is named the new—actually, the old—managing editor for the magazine.

▶ The only son of Ferdinand Marcos, president of the Philippines, takes fourth place at a local judo tourney.

▶ A practitioner of the Korean martial arts rails against *Black Belt's* frequent usage of Japanese terms, including *"taekwondo karate,"* to describe the Korean arts.

▶ A Parisian *judoka* strikes back at a man who would take liberties with her honor. The result: He gets a broken nose, dislocated wrist, bruised chin and sprained back. Her post-trial remark: "With judo, I can cool the most impetuous Casanova."

▶ When an irate reader complains that *Black Belt* hasn't featured a judoka on the cover in more than a year, the editor replies: "The covers are designed ... on the basis of past performance. We attempt to create the most appealing covers for the readers." Sounds like a formula for success.

▶ A Woodmere, New York, judo instructor reportedly refuses to accept an African-American student. The New York State Division of Human Rights schedules a hearing, but the grumpy grappler is a no-show. Apparently, he had no defense against the allegations.

▶ The high-kicking Radio City Music Hall Rockettes sign up for karate lessons to augment their dance routines.

▶ A practitioner of karate and kung fu turns pro boxer. "One of the hardest things for me to learn in boxing was *not* to block every punch," he says. "With bobbing and weaving, avoiding a punch is just as effective as blocking."

▶ When Hayward Nishioka travels to Mexico City to cover the World Judo Championships, he discovers that the Russians are as skilled at imbibing vodka as they are at choking and locking.

▶ Jigoro Kano, it's revealed, was so proud of his gams that he would frequently pull up his pant legs to show off his gargantuan calves.

▶ Travel warning: You might not want to study *Shaolin* kung fu in Singapore. A local martial artist writes, "It takes six months of daily practice to be able to withstand the beatings."

WORLD'S LEADING MAGAZINE OF SELF-DEFENSE

MARCH 1970 ⊠ 50 CENTS

BLACK BELT

YOU CAN'T LEARN KARATE IN TOURNEYS—Marchini

JAPAN DOMINATES MEXICO CITY'S WORLD JUDO TOURNEY

'DANGER IN KNUCKLE TOUGHENING' — ORTHOPEDIST WARNS

ISSUE SEVENTY-FIVE | MARCH 1970

The 75th issue of *Black Belt* was dated March 1970. It was 66 pages long and featured a photo of karate champion Ron Marchini on the cover.

Vol. 8, No. 3, 50 cents

▶ Reminding everyone of the political problems that ran rampant in the late 1960s and early '70s, a resident of New Haven, Connecticut, writes: "Mixing martial arts with law enforcement is like throwing water on a grease fire. ... The police are the state's right—sometimes ultraright—arm. ... Police can, and often do, function as tools of violence."

▶ In an unrelated development, Tak Kubota begins teaching hard-core karate to the Los Angeles Police Department.

▶ The clever marketing department at Martial Arts Supplies Company offers a small/medium "crotch guard" for $9 and a large/extra-large for $10.80. Knowing martial artists, it's a great way to earn an extra $1.80 per order.

▶ In his editorial, M. Uyehara decries the bestowing of honorary black belts, one of which was recently given to President Richard Nixon and another to John Wayne.

▶ *Matsubayashi* karate is officially established in Hawaii when Shoshin Nagamine pays the islands a visit.

▶ The University of Utah (Salt Lake City) opens its first for-credit judo class.

▶ In a rebuttal to an article lauding hand conditioning, a reader from Michigan writes: "It is of no use whatsoever. ... Your foot is your first defense, your knees and elbows second, and finally your hands."

▶ The big news of the month comes from a headline capping a tournament report: Japanese Dominate World Judo!

▶ Summing up the karate skills of the United States, Ron Marchini opines: "Easterners seem to like spinning back kicks. In the Midwest, they usually use the side-facing horse stance with the step-over back kick. To the north on the West Coast, they throw backhands and side kicks. In Southern California, the competitors are the most versatile."

▶ In the conclusion of his profile of judo founder Jigoro Kano, Andy Adams writes: "To Kano, a *kyudoka* was a judo man using a bow, and a *kendoka* was a judo man with a sword."

▶ *Black Belt's* resident bookworm takes a surgical look at *Your Personal Handbook of Self-Defense,* co-written by "Judo" Gene LeBell. His verdict? Thumbs down.

▶ After seeing a *Black Belt* cartoon of a *judoka* trying to throw a stubborn jackass, an irate grappler from the Soviet Union interrogates correspondent Hayward Nishioka because a nearby photo shows a competitor trying to toss the Russian with the same technique.

▶ In a letter shredding the recent North Georgia Karate Championship, Sol Freeman of Atlanta writes: "None of the judges or referees wore a karate suit. Joe Corley, chief referee, wore 'hippie' hair and pants."

▶ A Singapore-based martial artist attacks all the Shaolin posers teaching in his city-state: "There are too many masters of the various schools under the Shaolin banner."

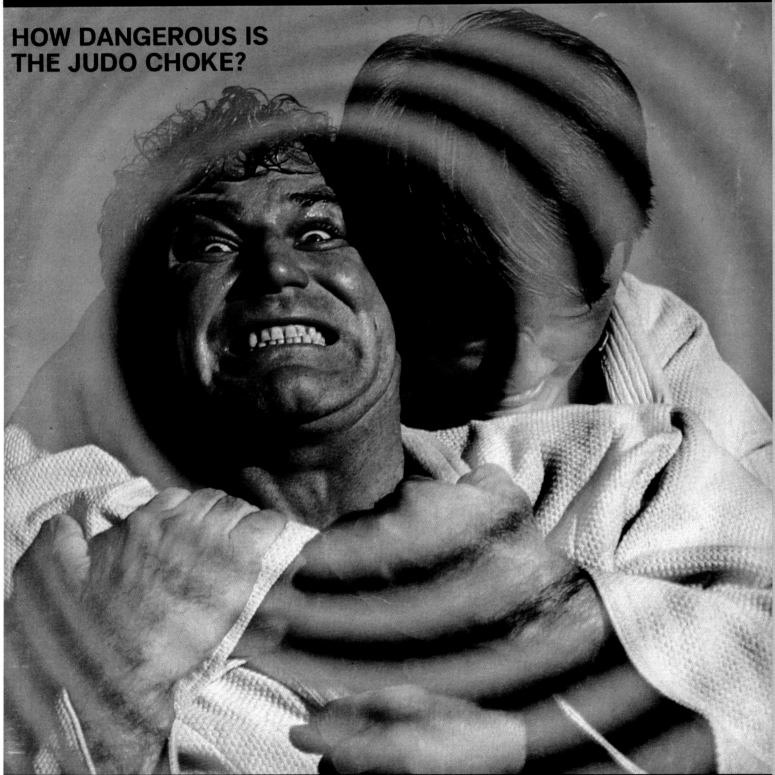

WORLD'S LEADING MAGAZINE OF SELF-DEFENSE

APRIL 1970 ✕ 50 CENTS

BLACK BELT

HOW DANGEROUS IS THE JUDO CHOKE?

MAS OYAMA'S WILDEST KARATE TOURNEY!

The 76th issue of *Black Belt* was dated April 1970. It was 66 pages long and featured a color photo of Hayward Nishioka choking Igor Zatsepin on the cover.

Vol. 8, No. 4, 50 cents

► Karate champ Mitchell Bobrow, who would go on to found a successful martial arts apparel company named Otomix, offers some insightful observations on his competition: "Chuck [Norris'] strongest armor is his experience in the ring. He is by far the smartest fighter today. Skipper [Mullins] probably has the fastest and most imaginative kicks in karate. Ron [Marchini] has the best counter in the game. Joe [Lewis] protects himself well while attacking. His chief weapons are the side kick and reverse punch, but few experts mention that [he] grabs and spins his opponent before he punches, and that is what makes his reverse punch so successful."

► Ed Parker announces he'll begin selling franchises of Ed Parker's Kenpo Karate Studios.

► When a reader takes Fumio Demura to task over the supposedly weak way he's holding a *sai* in a *Black Belt* photo, the good-natured karate master agrees with the observation, then replies: "When you have spent many hours manipulating the sai, you will understand that even a master is but a student of circumstance."

► A polished red-oak kung fu straight sword sells for $7.85.

► Three teenagers in the Philippines fall during their hike up the Mayon volcano. Two, who happen to be *judoka*, live, while the third dies. The survivors credit their *dojo*-learned rolling and tumbling skills for having saved their lives.

► South Korea's Defense Ministry sends several army *taekwondo* experts to Iran to beef up the Shah's guerrilla-warfare program.

► After conducting a scientific study of the physiology of judo chokes, the Kodokan concludes that while it can be dangerous to perform them on people with cardiac disorders, people suffering from hypertension and children, the techniques are "quite harmless" when used under the supervision of a qualified instructor on others who have trained in judo.

► At the first All-Japan Open Karate Tournament, a team of Thai boxers fares well even though its members are forced to fight under karate rules.

► Disgruntled cigarette-smoking former judo champ Taizu Noguchi lambastes the American interpretation of his art: "The United States is 30 years behind Japan and Europe. American *sensei* are too commercial. They are too easy on their students."

► *Shukokai* karate stylist Peter Consterdine is among the *kumite* winners at the United Kingdom Open Championships. Thirty-six years later, he'll be on *Black Belt's* list of the toughest men in the martial arts.

► A Filipino huckster is exposed for selling a course that purportedly teaches a rare Philippine art that comes from Japan, where it was learned from the Chinese, who in turn borrowed it from the Tibetans.

► *Karate Illustrated, Black Belt's* sister publication, goes monthly with its coverage of the exploding sport-karate world.

► Chuck Norris takes some flack for appearing in an after-shave commercial on television. His critics believe it will harm the reputation of the *budo*.

WORLD'S LEADING MAGAZINE OF SELF-DEFENSE

MAY 1970 50 CENTS

BLACK BELT

'BURSTING' ATTACK-POWER
OF CHICAGO'S KNUDSEN

'KENDO IS
ROUGHER
THAN KARATE'
Says Swordsman
Extraordinaire

ISSUE SEVENTY-SEVEN | MAY 1970

The 77th issue of *Black Belt* was dated May 1970. It was 66 pages long and featured a color photo of Ken Knudsen demonstrating "bursting power" on the cover.

Vol. 8, No. 5, 50 cents

▶ Chuck Norris quits competition so he can concentrate on teaching and promoting tournaments.

▶ To boost spectator turnout, the United States Karate Association Grand National Karate Championship hires four gyrating go-go dancers. More than 3,000 show up to gawk. Mike Foster wins top honors, but no one seems to care.

▶ Sumo champ Taiho racks up a phenomenal 663 wins in his career.

▶ It's 1970, and still the martial arts world is debating the pros and cons of supplementing *dojo* training with weightlifting.

▶ A reader from Berkeley, California, reveals that before World War I, German chemists analyzed a Japanese sword forged in 1330 and found it was made of molybdenum steel, which was ultra high-tech for the era.

▶ If you're a size 5, you can get a pair of judo *gi* pants for less than $5. A sleek judo supporter will cost you $2.

▶ Weight Watchers helps the "world's biggest black belt," aka Jim Jackson, drop from 396 pounds to 261 pounds. His motivation? His *sensei* attempted to throw him in competition and ended up spraining his back.

▶ His may not be a household name, but *goju-shorei* stylist Ken Knudsen is earning a reputation as a solid performer on the circuit, having defeated Bill Wallace, Louis Delgado and John Norman.

▶ Need accident insurance for your dojo? Prepare to cough up $16 a year.

▶ "Tournament karate is destroying the art and turning it into just another sport," laments a reader from Van Nuys, California, who was just disillusioned by the monetary demands of a would-be instructor.

▶ "It is my belief that no karate fighter could stand the battering a *kendo* man must endure in a kendo match," says Yoshiteru Otani, a sword master based in New York.

▶ Candidate for the Understatement of the Year Award: Professor Seidler of California State University reportedly sees Bruce Lee punching and says, "In three years, you can be a world boxing champion." He watches Lee spar and says, "In two years, you can be a world [karate] champion." Then he spies Lee hitting a punching pad and says, "In one year, you can become a champ."

▶ A reader takes *Black Belt's* Japan correspondent, Andy Adams, to task over some controversial historical statements he made. The reader's name is ... Louis L'Amour?

WORLD'S LEADING MAGAZINE OF SELF-DEFENSE

JUNE 1970 50 CENTS

BLACK BELT

FIGHTING TEXANS BALK AT BEGINNING KARATE
—Pat Burleson

FRICTION FRACTURES UNITED STATES JUDO

I S S U E S E V E N T Y - E I G H T | J U N E 1 9 7 0

The 78th issue of *Black Belt* was dated June 1970. It was 66 pages long and featured a color photo of Pat Burleson—dubbed a "portrait of double-fisted fury"—on the cover.

Vol. 8, No. 6, 50 cents

▶ Bruce Lee closes his school in Los Angeles' Chinatown, leaving his students to train with Dan Inosanto.

▶ George Dillman pledges the proceeds from his fourth annual Northeast U.S. Karate Tournament to his local National Guard Armory, where he serves as a lieutenant.

▶ On opposite coasts, two legends open ultra-luxurious *dojo.* Chuck Norris occupies 6,000 square feet in Torrance, California, and Jhoon Rhee acquires 4,000 square feet in Washington, D.C.

▶ The only woman in a judo course at Stanford University makes the news when she forgets to remove her wig before *randori* and her opponent unknowingly snatches it right off her head.

▶ When rowdy black belts get ready to rumble at a Trenton, New Jersey, karate tournament, promoter Preston Carter responds by canceling the finals, returning the registration fees and passing out trophies to all who won their elimination bouts.

▶ Chuck Sereff heads the rapidly expanding karate program at the U.S. Air Force Academy in Colorado Springs, Colorado.

▶ Pat Burleson reminisces about the early days of karate competition: "We had almost no techniques for close quarters. We just grabbed our opponent and tried to tackle him."

▶ Ever wonder how *shime waza,* the strangling techniques of judo, work? Dr. Leonard I. Lapinsohn offers some insight: "Strangles place direct pressure on both the carotid and vertebral arteries. Lowered brain circulation is effected directly ... when ... pressure is gradually increased. If external pressure is ... suddenly released, the surge of pressure will cause reflex changes resulting in marked systemic blood-pressure drop, faintness, weakness or unconsciousness."

▶ At Allen Steen's eighth annual United States Karate Championships, five high-profile martial artists serve as referees: Skipper Mullins, Jack Hwang, Ed Parker, Kang Rhee and Kim Soo. More than 1,000 competitors and 8,000 spectators show up to watch Fred Wren take the grand championship.

▶ What's the best way to train for judo? A Russian champ and controversial coach known as Anderyev says the secret of his team's success is cross-training in soccer, basketball, running, swimming, gymnastics, wrestling and *sambo.*

▶ Kim Jae-joon is appointed head of the American Moo Duk Kwan Association.

▶ At the second annual U.S. International Karate Championships in Miami, Mike Foster stuns 3,000-plus onlookers when he withdraws from the finals before his bout with Louis Delgado. His excuse? He has to catch a plane.

WORLD'S LEADING MAGAZINE OF SELF-DEFENSE

JULY 1970 · 50 CENTS

BLACK BELT

JHOON RHEE:
The Pied Piper
of Korean Karate

'KENJAH'—Headhunters'
Tribal Art of Murder

ISSUE SEVENTY-NINE | JULY 1970

The 79th issue of *Black Belt* was dated July 1970. It was 66 pages long and featured a color photo of Jhoon Rhee on the cover.

Vol. 8, No. 7, 50 cents

▶ Bruce Lee is on the go. After visiting the Caribbean, he jets to London and Switzerland, then Japan and Hong Kong. During his trip, a Greek millionaire reportedly offers him $1,000 an hour for private lessons. Lee declines because he's busy working on a movie script with Stirling Silliphant and James Coburn.

▶ An enterprising reader from Maryland writes: "I have been distributing unsold copies of *Black Belt* to barbershops, restaurants and doctor's offices in the vicinity of my karate school. Stapling an ad for my school to the inside cover and circling my listing in the Dojo Directory is a thrifty way to advertise." We're in!

▶ A stink is raised when Korean *taekwondo* master Son Duk Sung gives an honorary black belt to President Richard Nixon.

▶ Future *Black Belt* Hall of Fame member Jhoon Rhee prepares to hold his second annual Karate Kamp in Chesapeake Bay, Maryland.

▶ The number of taekwondo practitioners in America is estimated to fall between 250,000 and 300,000.

▶ A German *judoka* is arrested on charges of spying for the Soviet Union.

▶ A TV series composed of 130 five-minute episodes is launched in Hollywood. Its name? *Self-Defense for Women.* (No relation to the magazine this company would publish 33 years later.)

▶ A Big Apple resident claims that the karate techniques being taught to modern students are virtually worthless on the street. "Kicks and eye strikes do not block knives and sticks," he writes. No, his name is not Jim Wagner.

▶ The remote islands that make up Fiji recently got their own karate club. It now boasts 38 members.

▶ Korean stylist and tourney champ Joe Hayes opines: "There's something disrespectful about a karate man accepting money for a bout in the same way as a professional boxer."

▶ Recovering from a disastrous 1969 event that attracted only a few hundred competitors, S. Henry Cho's All-American Championship bounces back in 1970 and draws in excess of 1,500. William Swift takes top honors.

▶ Prepubescent boys in Borneo learn a bizarre blade art/martial dance called *kenjah.* It's all part of growing up, they say.

▶ Ten years after arriving in the United States with only $400 to his name, Jhoon Rhee oversees a chain of five successful East Coast schools, has a student base of 800 and lives in a huge home in an affluent neighborhood.

▶ Bill Wallace places first at the Michigan Invitational Karate Championships.

▶ A dearth of damsels at the University of California, Berkeley, karate club prompts a group of disgruntled women to storm the men's locker room and demand "Self-defense for women now!" The menaced men relent and promise an all-female karate class next semester.

WORLD'S LEADING MAGAZINE OF SELF-DEFENSE

AUGUST 1970 ✦ 50 CENTS

BLACK BELT

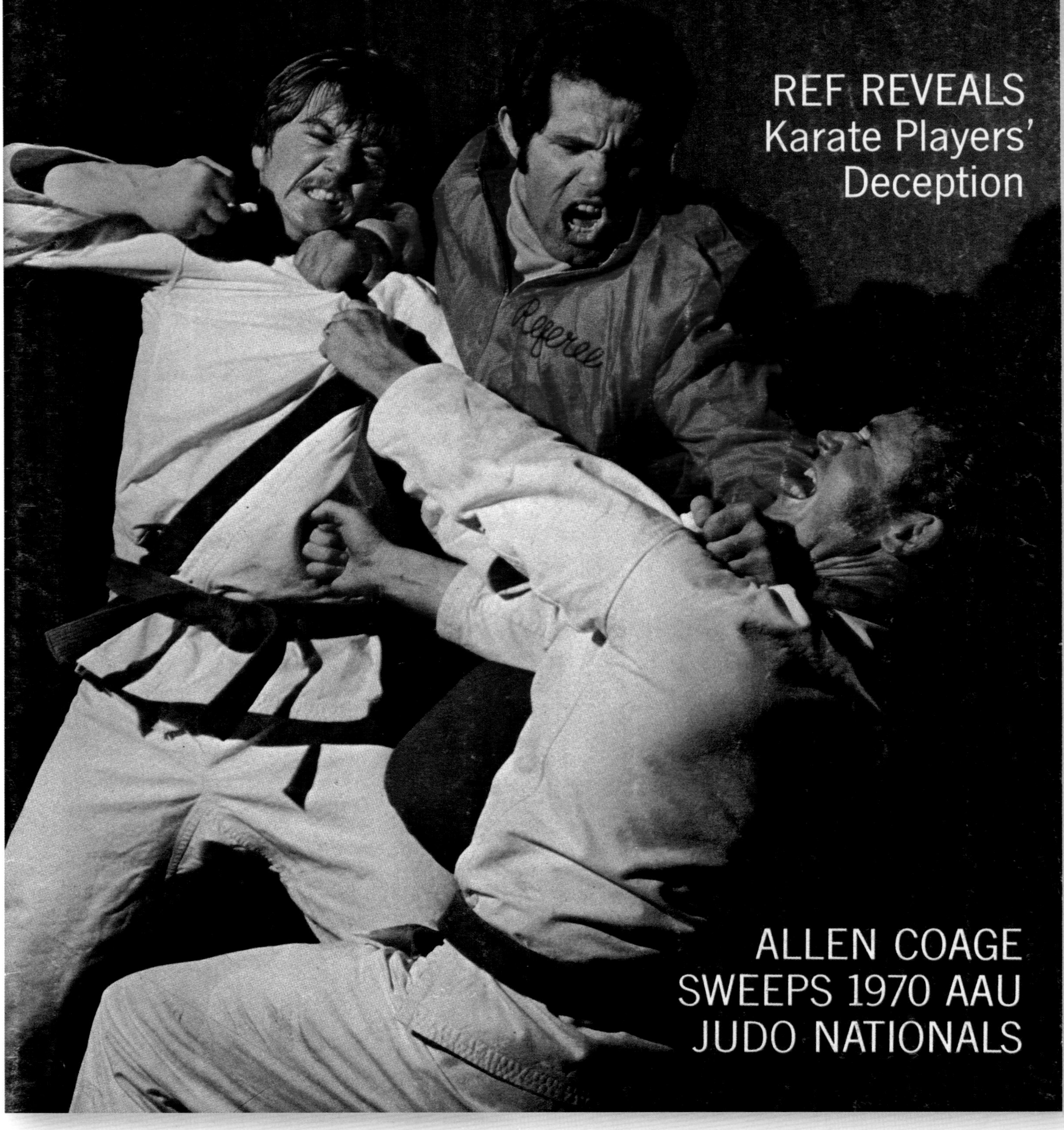

REF REVEALS
Karate Players'
Deception

ALLEN COAGE
SWEEPS 1970 AAU
JUDO NATIONALS

ISSUE EIGHTY | AUGUST 1970

The 80th issue of *Black Belt* was dated August 1970. It was 66 pages long and featured a color photo of Bobby Burbidge, Pat Johnson and John Thawley (left to right) on the cover.

Vol. 8, No. 8, 50 cents

▶ During a visit to Hong Kong, Bruce Lee is surprised to see himself in reruns of *The Green Hornet*—with a dubbed-in Chinese voice.

▶ *Dojo* wars heat up in Chicago, where students of the Black Cobra Hall of Kung Fu Kempo and the House of (Count) Dante rumble. One man is stabbed to death, and another sustains a severe eye injury.

▶ *Black Belt* begins selling posters of its most popular cover paintings. Measuring 25 inches by 31 inches, they go for $1.95 apiece.

▶ Defending himself against accusations that the talent level at his tournaments isn't quite up to par, Aaron Banks fires back with a list of fighters who've done battle in his Big Apple show: Chuck Norris, Mike Stone, Joe Lewis, Wally Slocki, Louis Delgado, Skipper Mullins, Ray Martin and so on.

▶ The progenitor of the modern training dummy—a headless, armless canvas cylinder with legs and a reinforced crotch—hits the market at $55.95.

▶ At the Second Jayhawk Karate Tournament, Walt Lang endures a knockout and six stitches.

▶ Korean Airlines begins stationing a judo expert on every overseas flight in an effort to prevent another hijacking by North Korean agents.

▶ In his critique of karate tournaments, future *Black Belt* Hall of Fame member Pat Johnson opines: "The audience and officials might overlook the first point scored because it happens so fast. Too often, the second point is landed only because of a reflex action. Then the first point is forgotten."

▶ John Saxon, future co-star of *Enter the Dragon,* switches from karate to *tai chi chuan.*

▶ The 1970 National AAU Judo Championships in Anaheim, California, attract nearly 3,000 spectators and competitors. Standouts include Hayward Nishioka, Allen Coage and Pat Burris.

▶ Following a campaign against TV violence, ABC's *Wide World of Sports* discontinues its coverage of martial arts tournaments.

▶ *Life* magazine estimates that the number of female *judoka* in the United States has risen from 500 to 20,000 in the past decade.

▶ Joe Lewis takes the grand championship at the 1970 Southeast U.S. Open Karate Championship.

WORLD'S LEADING MAGAZINE OF SELF-DEFENSE

SEPTEMBER 1970 50 CENTS

BLACK BELT

"SOME AIKIDO TECHNIQUES ARE VULNERABLE,
BUT KARATE MAKES THEM WORK"
— Dan Ivan's Hybrid Self-Defense

THE JUDO SPLIT AFTERMATH—A POLL OF PROMINENT JUDOKA

ISSUE EIGHTY-ONE | SEPTEMBER 1970

The 81st issue of *Black Belt* was dated September 1970. It was 66 pages long and featured a color photo of Dan Ivan on the cover.

Vol. 8, No. 9, 50 cents

▶ In Malaysia, 60-year-old *tai chi* expert Huang Sheng Hsien takes on wrestling champion Leow Kong Seng. After five three-minute rounds, Huang has scored 26 points (via throws) to his opponent's zero.

▶ An American martial artist travels to Israel and finds *Black Belt* and its sister publication, *Karate Illustrated,* plastered all over the nation's newsstands.

▶ Publisher M. Uyehara examines the divide that's growing in the American martial arts community: "[The person] making a living from the arts says he can't teach properly if he can't give his full effort to the arts, which means a full-time job. The part-timer says that no one should make a dime teaching the arts because otherwise he'll place money before the arts. We take a stand in between."

▶ The city of Penang, Malaysia, hosts the Martial Arts Expo '70. A number of arts— including karate, judo, *bersilat,* kung fu, *selambam,* Thai dancing and archery—are demonstrated for a capacity crowd.

▶ A red-oak kung fu practice sword sells for $9.25. Thirty-six years later, the same item costs, on average, $19.

▶ During a sumo demonstration in Australia, a boy spies the thong-clad competitors and tells his mother, "Look, those gentlemen have forgotten to put their pants on."

▶ Dan Ivan, a pioneer in the Japanese martial arts, recalls the early days of the arts in America: "No one knew what *aikido* was. We had to call everything 'judo.' Once the public was in, we could teach them anything, whether it was aikido, karate or whatever."

▶ After winning the West Coast Judo Championships, Hayward Nishioka finds his visit to Japan an eye-opener. "I thought I was pretty good … and I was going to show those Japanese judo men some top American techniques," he says. "After five minutes of *randori,* I didn't have a chance to show them anything. They were too busy proving to me how great they really were."

▶ In the semifinals of the 1970 Universal Open Karate Championships and Tournament of Champions, Joe Hayes battles Bob Engle for a grueling 20 minutes. Hayes wins the bout— and goes on to defeat Joe Corley for the title.

▶ Ohara Publications (now called Black Belt Books) prepares to release its newest title, *Ninja: The Invisible Assassins,* by Andy Adams.

▶ In a sign of the times, a reader voices his thoughts on *Black Belt's* cartoons: "I enjoy your magazine, but one thing bothers me. The bad guy or 'hood' is always represented as a hippie or someone wearing a peace symbol."

▶ A new regime in Burma vows to fight suppression of the rare martial art of *myanmar lethwai.*

WORLD'S LEADING MAGAZINE OF SELF-DEFENSE

OCTOBER 1970 50 CENTS

BLACK BELT

KARATE YOUNGSTER'S
NEW TWISTS ON
OLD PHILOSOPHIES

SELAMBAM: INDIAN
STICK FIGHTING ART

JUDO CHAMPIONSHIPS: RUSSIA REIGNS IN EUROPE; MEIJI U. TAKES ALL-JAPAN

ISSUE EIGHTY-TWO | OCTOBER 1970

The 82nd issue of *Black Belt* was dated October 1970. It was 66 pages long and featured a color photo of Jeff Klein on the cover.

Vol. 8, No. 10, 50 cents

▶ Willie Norris, Chuck Norris' brother and the second-place finisher at the 1969 International Karate Championships, passes away after being shot by a North Vietnamese sniper.

▶ At a meeting of the Amateur Athletic Union Judo Committee, it's decided that "any hair below the angle of the lips and traced to the angle of the jaw is considered to be a beard and will not be allowed." Likewise, follicles that overlap the ears or the collar are unacceptable.

▶ In the Indian stick-fighting art of *selambam,* students are taught to never lift both feet off the ground at the same time. Such leaps, it's believed, lead to a loss of control and leave the practitioner open to counterattack.

▶ Need a stationary bicycle for the *dojo*? It'll cost you $54.95. A deluxe model goes for $64.95.

▶ Bruce Lee announces a casting call for martial artists interested in participating in his upcoming film *The Silent Flute*. Academy Award-winning screenwriter Stirling Silliphant and leading-man James Coburn are already on board.

▶ Misguided do-gooders in the Florida Legislature introduce a bill that would ban anyone under the age of 16 from studying the Asian arts of self-defense.

▶ Former All-Japan karate champ Chuzo Kotaka quietly sets up shop in Hawaii. Thus begins the reign of the Kotaka family and their students, who still rule the martial arts community of the Pacific.

▶ *Taekwondo* legend-in-the-making Hee Il Cho wins the Midwest Open Invitational Karate Tournament in Rockford, Illinois.

▶ Jeff Klein, a 17-year-old student of karate great Tsutomu Ohshima, lives the *bushido* ideal. "One of the most important decisions a man must make in life is to be prepared for death," Klein says. "It is through this preparation for death that he can truly be free."

▶ A subscription to *Black Belt*—that's 12 issues plus the yearbook—costs $5.75.

▶ A New York *goju-ryu* karate black belt proclaims, "I have been attacked many times by a number of men, and I have always been able to defend myself as I was taught by my instructor."

▶ A Texas newsman laments the lack of positive coverage of the martial arts: "The only time you see anything about karate in the papers is when something terrible happens, like the recent Chicago killing or when a group from the Women's Liberation starts training to beat up their husbands."

WORLD'S LEADING MAGAZINE OF SELF-DEFENSE — NOVEMBER 1970 50 CENTS

BLACK BELT

LEO FONG EXPOSES WEAKNESSES
IN MAJOR FIGHTING STYLES

AIKIDO
THE PACIFIST'S ART

ISSUE EIGHTY-THREE | NOVEMBER 1970

The 83rd issue *of Black Belt* was dated November 1970. It was 66 pages long and featured a color photo of Leo Fong on the cover.

Vol. 8, No. 11, 50 cents

► A reader from Groves, Texas, opines about rank: "Most Oriental countries seem to give the impression that they have complete ownership of martial arts knowledge and can dole out it and rank at their pleasure. By the way, how did the first person of high rank obtain it if there was no one above him to promote him?"

► Kim Yong Choi, president of the Korea Taekwondo Association, travels to Southeast Asia to evaluate how well his art is being spread there.

► "There are no bouts in *aikido,*" New York's Yoshimitsu Yamada says, "because bouts only fatten the egos of the winners. Competition adds nothing and completely destroys the humility concept of *bushido.*"

► Cover-subject Leo Fong describes an incident from his childhood: "I found a book on boxing and studied it from cover to cover in my room at night. Then one day, I had a chance to try it out. It was in my fifth-grade English class, and another kid called me 'ching-chong Chinaman.' I stood up and cold-cocked him right there."

► Dr. Maung Gyi sponsors the first International Martial Sports Exhibition in Ohio. More than 3,000 fans show up to watch the matches and demos.

► A Southern California-based *karateka* takes Chuck Norris to task over an ad campaign Norris' schools are running in the *Los Angeles Times:* "One ad shows the shapely legs of a girl with the caption, 'Would a girl with legs like this waste her time doing karate?' The ads talk about 'keeping your figure trim and slim' and 'having a ball.' They boast of their sauna and steam baths, ladies' hair dryers, showers and lockers. This is *budo?*"

► Norris replies: "Showing a girl's legs is not harmful. What we are trying to explain is that a woman does not develop legs like a fullback on a football team but that karate does truly develop them firm and trim. I guess my students do, as you say, have a ball in their training. I believe karate training should be rigorous and enjoyable. And we do have sauna baths for the students to soothe their sore muscles."

► A Canadian karate instructor gets nabbed for rigging a tournament lottery in which he offered two plane tickets to Japan but didn't deliver. His take: $860.

► Penning his last *Black Belt* column before passing away, Dr. Leonard I. Lapinsohn extols the virtues of *tai chi*—with a warning: "Tai chi is excellent for cardiac patients if done under medical supervision. As an aid in psychiatric treatment, it is of extreme value. I wish to state, however, that some of the claims made [about tai chi] are based on what the Chinese call 'wild history,' a type of record that is not deemed trustworthy. The classical Chinese medical explanations for some of the effects are also unacceptable in light of current scientific and medical knowledge."

► At a karate and judo tournament in the Philippines, the gymnasium floor caves in. More than 80 martial artists and spectators are injured.

► *Time* magazine profiles the women's liberation movement, noting that karate is popular among its members.

► After Jhoon Rhee's demo team struts its stuff on the White House lawn, first lady Pat Nixon quips, "Good luck to all of you—and don't come around me; you know too much."

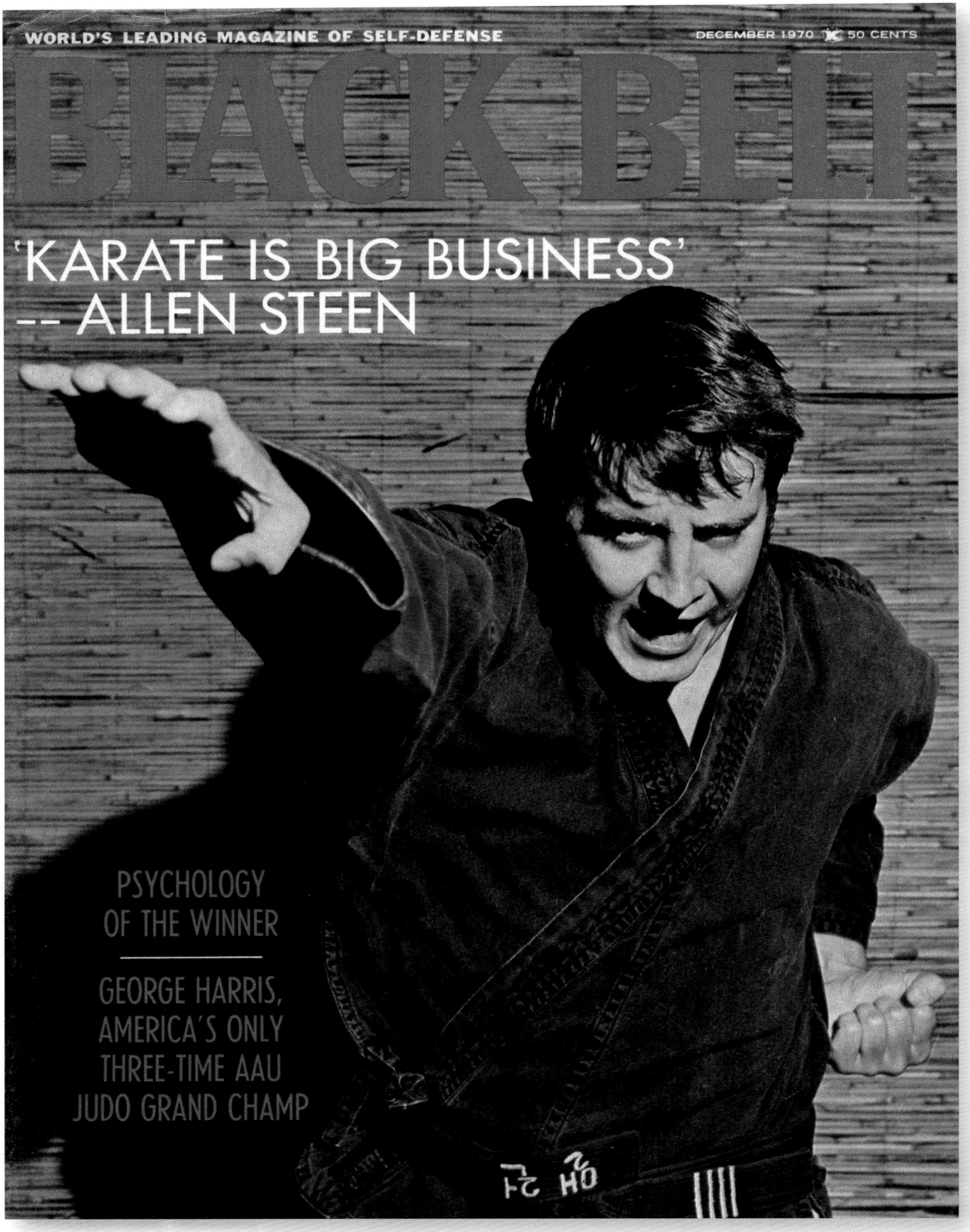

WORLD'S LEADING MAGAZINE OF SELF-DEFENSE
DECEMBER 1970 50 CENTS
BLACK BELT
'KARATE IS BIG BUSINESS'
-- ALLEN STEEN
PSYCHOLOGY
OF THE WINNER
GEORGE HARRIS,
AMERICA'S ONLY
THREE-TIME AAU
JUDO GRAND CHAMP

ISSUE EIGHTY-FOUR | DECEMBER 1970

The 84th issue of *Black Belt* was dated December 1970. It was 66 pages long and featured a color photo of Allen Steen on the cover.

Vol. 8, No. 12, 50 cents

► On the record: "Several years ago, we announced that Bruce Lee was working on a book called *Tao of Jeet Kune Do*," *Black Belt* reports. "Unfortunately, Bruce got sidetracked from writing it, and even though it was almost completed, he has decided not to have it published." The martial arts world is pleased that things turned out otherwise.

► "Karate as a sport is flourishing, while the art is dying," another reader writes. "It is my belief that unless something is done soon, the word *kata* will become unfamiliar. After all, what is karate without kata?"

► John W. Zeck debunks the ever-popular stunt in which a master lies on a bed of nails while an assistant places a rock on his stomach and smashes it with a sledgehammer: "Although one nail pressed against a fingertip may puncture the skin, if your weight is spread evenly over a bed of many nails, you may rest quite comfortably, providing you don't move. And the larger the stone or other object to be broken, the more it will absorb the impact of the blow and the less it will be felt by the person on the receiving end."

► The legendary Allen Steen reveals his thoughts on the classical-versus-commercial war that's erupting in the karate world: "First, a classical school does not have the money to buy the best equipment. Second, it cannot afford to attract large numbers of people and develop a high breed of karate player. Next, it cannot afford to go to tournaments in other states."

► A happy reader from Orange, California, opines: "[The article about Dan Ivan] in the September 1970 issue was a penetrating study of one of the most unheralded men in American karate."

► The staff of *Black Belt* readies its 1970 Yearbook for the newsstand. *Kyokushin* karate's Mas Oyama will grace the cover.

► French *savate* champ Christian Guillaume blazes a trail through the Land of the Rising Sun when he defeats five Japanese kickboxers in five matches.

► More from Allen Steen: "The most thrilling match I ever had was for the grand championship against Chuck Norris. There were about 12,000 to 15,000 people there. A lot of them were for me, but a lot more were for Norris. I really had to work to win that match. But I have never faced a tougher competitor than Joe Lewis. He has a good defense and is very fast with a dynamic power."

► Editor M. Uyehara weighs in on the subject of karate competition in America: "A student will not retain his interest in the arts without competition. This is why *jujutsu* has almost become extinct in Japan but judo has flourished throughout the world. This is why karate has become so popular while *aikido* has remained so docile."

► At the United States Karate Association Grand Nationals in Anderson, Indiana, Bill Wallace does the unthinkable: After five rounds of action, he defeats Joe Lewis and walks away with his title. In the event's kata competition, George Dillman nabs first.

► In the latest round of the battle of the sexes, the ladies lash out at the male martial artists of the University of California, Berkeley, with slurs like "chauvinist karate freaks."

► "When you enter a tournament and lose, whom do you blame?" asks future *Black Belt* Hall of Fame member Hayward Nishioka. "Competitors of any high level of proficiency usually know whom to blame: themselves. It is persons of a lesser degree of skill who blame the referee or the opponent." Sounds like good advice to us.

WORLD'S LEADING MAGAZINE OF SELF-DEFENSE

JANUARY 1971 ✕ 60 CENTS

BLACK BELT

PAT WORLEY IS HIS
OWN WORST CRITIC

JUDO'S GRAND OLD
MAN, MEL BRUNO

HANG-UPS OF
A CHAMP

BLACK BELT MAGAZINE
10th
ANNIVERSARY

Issue Eighty-Five | January 1971

The 85th issue of *Black Belt* was dated January 1971. It was 66 pages long and featured a color photo of Pat Worley on the cover.

Vol. 9, No. 1, 60 cents

▶ In celebrating *Black Belt's* 10th anniversary, editor M. Uyehara looks back on some of the competing magazines that have fallen by the wayside: *Judo Digest, Judo Journal, New England Judo News, Judo World* and, ahem, *Red Belt.*

▶ After spending three weeks Down Under, *goju-ryu* karate legend Gogen Yamaguchi proclaims, "Australians are strong and have a very sound technical knowledge of the art."

▶ The going rate for karate lessons in Minnesota is $10 a month.

▶ Spain boasts 15,000 practicing *judoka,* including 400 male black belts and 10 female black belts.

▶ "Tournaments are a testing ground for how hard one has worked and how determined one is to win," says Pat Worley, a 21-year-old Texan educated in Washington, D.C., by the great Jhoon Rhee. "If I lose, it means that I haven't worked out enough. I have no one to blame but myself."

▶ In Yugoslavia, women score a point for equal rights. Female judoka now compete under the same rules as men—which means ground work, arm locks and strangulation techniques are allowed.

▶ "If physical activity is used only to build the body, it is called physical education. However, if physical activity is used for living, it is called a means for the elevation of life." Those are the words of judo founder Jigoro Kano.

▶ A high-quality, double-weave judo *gi* costs $15.50. Add two bucks if you need a "special judo supporter" to go along with it.

▶ *Black Belt* profiles Mel Bruno, the American martial arts pioneer who was the first to teach judo to California's prison guards. Previously, Bruno swapped ideas with *shotokan* karate founder Gichin Funakoshi during a trip to Japan.

▶ One thousand fans attend the Asian Festival of Combat Sports in Manila, Philippines. Among the arts represented are karate, *aikido, taekwondo,* wrestling, Thai boxing, *sambo,* fencing, *Shaolin* kung fu, sword fighting and, of course, modern *arnis,* courtesy of Remy Presas.

▶ At the 1970 California Capital Karate Championships, hosted by Ron Marchini, Leo Fong and Dan Babcock, Chuck Norris leads his team of black belts to victory. Al Dacascos takes first in the lightweight *kumite* division.

▶ Meanwhile, Joe Lewis KO's Ed Daniel 38 seconds into round two of their match at the USA Open Pro Karate Championships.

▶ Students who sign up for lessons at Kimbrell's New Age School for Self-Defense in San Francisco can expect something a little different. "We don't have to break boards," Neville Kimbrell says. "We don't emphasize belt ranking, just study, and we don't enter the arena of ego tournaments. Those people into yoga, meditation and natural foods will find that karate is part of the same trip."

WORLD'S LEADING MAGAZINE OF SELF-DEFENSE

FEBRUARY 1971   50 CENTS

BLACK BELT

HAROLD GROSS'
WINNING BEAT

COLLEGIATE
JUDO'S
TREACHEROUS
TRIANGLE

ISSUE EIGHTY-SIX | FEBRUARY 1971

The 86th issue of *Black Belt* was dated February 1971. It was 66 pages long and featured a color photo of Harold Gross (punching) and Jay Friedman on the cover.

Vol. 9, No. 2, 50 cents

► After *Black Belt* reported that Bruce Lee had decided not to have his *Tao of Jeet Kune Do* published, martial artists launch a letter-writing campaign to convince him to change his mind.

► Cover boy Harold Gross reveals one of the secrets of his success: Using music to improve his reflexes for sparring.

► Mike Stone makes a surprise appearance at the All-States Open Karate Championship in Youngstown, Ohio, and takes top honors in the *kata* division.

► The 1970 *Black Belt* Hall of Fame inductees are announced: Eichi K. Koiwai, George Wilson, Ki Whang Kim, Shinichi Suzuki, Ark Y. Wong, Allen Coage and Ronald Marchini.

► Men, take note: The elegantly named Crotch Guard is now on sale. Smalls and mediums go for $10.40. No doubt the large and extra large are better sellers despite costing $2 more.

► Martial arts census report: Judo has existed in Athens, Greece, for 20 years, but during that time, it's managed to attract only 100 practitioners. Meanwhile, half a world away in South Korea, the Seoul YMCA services more than 2,600 *judoka*.

► *Black Belt* polls *aikido* instructors to divine the future of the art in America. Yukiso Yamamoto replies: "It is not growing as fast as some of the other martial arts due to the outstanding characteristics of aikido, [which] seeks first the development of *ki* and the control of mind. This is a very slow process."

► *Black Belt* book reviewer Dr. Philip J. Rasch sums up the fan mail he's received over the years: "[It] appears to delineate the personality of the *karateka* quite differently from that of the *judoka*. It presents the former as an individual who feels insecure in his environment. He learns a self-defense art and seeks an authority figure as his master. The judoka seems tougher-minded, more secure, so that he can devote his free time to a sport."

► Ninety karateka in Trinidad consider themselves fortunate when karate great Hirokazu Kanazawa arrives to teach a two-week clinic.

► "There are two types of judo," Jigoro Kano writes. "Small judo is concerned with only techniques and the building of the body. Large judo is mindful of the pursuit of the purpose of life: the soul and the body used in the most effective manner for a good result."

► In Brussels, Belgium, seven partying Japanese salarymen storm a nondescript building and, once inside, let loose a series of *kiai* and midair karate chops. They quickly realize they've made a mistake when the people working inside pick up machine guns and take aim. The building turns out to be a police station.

► The Northern District of the American Ju-Jitsu Institute of Hawaii, which strangely enough is based in Monterey, California, re-elects Willy Cahill as president and Wally Jay as secretary.

► Bill Wallace faces off against Glenn Keeney in the finals at the American Karate Association Championships. Wallace wins using one of the five techniques he's comfortable with: the side kick.

WORLD'S LEADING MAGAZINE OF SELF-DEFENSE

MARCH 1971   60 CENTS

BLACK BELT

TONNY TULLENERS: BEST U.S. KARATE FIGHTER TODAY

JUDO BREAKS INTO THE IVY LEAGUE

JAPAN CAPTURES FIRST WORLD KARATE CHAMPIONSHIP

JUDO'S FIGHTING NUNS

REVENGE OF THE BETRAYED WARRIOR

ISSUE EIGHTY-SEVEN | MARCH 1971

The 87th issue of *Black Belt* was dated March 1971. It was 66 pages long and featured a color photo of Tonny Tulleners on the cover.

Vol. 9, No. 3, 60 cents

▶ Kim Dan-hwa, a petite 23-year-old *hapkido* stylist from South Korea who's been dubbed "Miss Hercules," amazes audiences at home and in Japan with her demonstrations of internal energy and stamina. Among other feats, she tows a truck with her teeth and allows a male assistant to hammer her chest.

▶ A letter writer from North Hollywood references a Chinese master named Low Bung. Let's hope he's changed his name. ...

▶ A Japanese white-oak *kobudo nunchaku,* modeled by Fumio Demura in the ad, sells for $4.50.

▶ Having conquered the karate world, Mike Stone takes on football. He rallies his martial arts students, pits them against Chuck Norris' guys—and wins 26-18.

▶ Cover boy Tonny Tulleners serves up some of the wisdom of his winning ways: "The more I have a person backing away and off-balance, the more I pour it on and the less of a chance he has of recovering. It's when you stop or slow down that you give him an opportunity to recover."

▶ When a group of New Orleans nuns enlists at a judo school, chaos ensues. "My folks were awed, but not [because of] my enrollment in judo," one says with a blush. "They said they could see my underwear under my habit."

▶ John Green from Australia writes to congratulate American martial artists: "To the average Aussie, the American is regarded as a braggart and poser. But after seeing some American *karateka* and *judoka* in action, they aren't to be laughed at or looked down upon. These people are to be respected."

▶ Korean master Hwang In-soo, a sixth-degree black belt, joins the faculty of Yale University and launches a comprehensive judo program.

▶ Breaking news from Hollywood: Warner Bros. is planning to film *Kung Fu,* a story about an 18th-century monk trained in the fighting arts. So far, there's no word on who will star. David Carradine, mail in your head shots now.

▶ Stirling Silliphant states in a *Variety* interview that his upcoming pic, *The Silent Flute,* "may be the most violent film ever made."

▶ A 13-issue subscription to *Black Belt* costs $5.75, while a 12-issue sub to sister publication *Karate Illustrated* runs $6.50.

▶ An animal lover from Dayton, Ohio, takes a potshot at Mas Oyama for his barehanded bouts with bulls. "Killing a bull is something many strong men could do," he opines. "Bulls are not as agile as a man nor are they as bright."

WORLD'S LEADING MA— SELF-DEFENSE   APRIL 1971   60 CENTS

BLACK BELT

WRESTLERS REVEAL
FLAWS IN JUDO

AGE IS NO
BARRIER
TO KARATE

MISSION:
ASSASSINATION

ISSUE EIGHTY-EIGHT | APRIL 1971

The 88th issue of *Black Belt* was dated April 1971. It was 66 pages long and featured a color photo of Jim West (lifting *judoka* Bob Sheppard) on the cover.

Vol. 9, No. 4, 60 cents

▶ Apparently, the Chinese aren't the only ones who tried to keep their fighting arts to themselves. Editor M. Uyehara reports that before World War II, the Japanese attempted to do the same thing with judo.

▶ A Brooklyn, New York-based reader railing against the commercialization of the martial arts asks, "If students have a ball working out, are they truly learning karate?"

▶ Future *Black Belt* Hall of Fame member Leo Fong goes to bat for a student who KO'd his foe in a tournament but never received the promised prize of $25.

▶ Already a legend, *taekwondo* instructor Jhoon Rhee releases *Tan-Gun and To-San of Tae Kwon Do Hyung*. Thirty-six years later, the book is still in print.

▶ A reader from—where else?—California writes to complain about the discrimination he and his "fellow longhairs" are experiencing in the *dojo*.

▶ At age 73, Sen. Milton R. Young, R-N.D., busts a board with a knifehand blow as Jhoon Rhee holds the pine.

▶ After a failed attempt to take over his nation's government, a renowned Japanese novelist/martial artist commits suicide the only way he knows how: by *seppuku,* the ritualized abdominal cut, which he performs in public with a $10,000 blade.

▶ In Denmark, the minister of education bans women and girls from participating in self-defense training. The reason? He fears the "uncontrolled and brutal practices" of karate might find their way into the classes.

▶ At a round-table discussion designed to determine why judo in America isn't as popular as wrestling, Jim West weighs in on the age issue: "Even if [a wrestling champion] is 50, we should keep him on the mat until someone else can come along and beat him."

▶ Book reviewer Dr. Philip J. Rasch tempts fate by reporting that *Ninja,* by Andrew Adams, "suffers from a surprisingly large amount of redundancy. The need for closer editorial control is obvious." The thing is, the book is published by Ohara Publications, the sister company of *Black Belt.*

▶ Al Dacascos becomes the grand champion at the Central North American Karate Championship after he defeats Travis Everitt.

▶ An Air Force sergeant who has trained extensively in Asia says, "I've seen Thai boxers knock the stuff out of men twice [Joe] Lewis' size and ability. ... I think kickboxing will destroy the martial arts, and it should be stopped before it spreads and death results."

▶ Need a leather double-buckle wrist brace—you know, the kind that makes you look tough? You can pick one up for $1.90. (Word of warning: They weren't cool then, and they're not cool now.)

WORLD'S LEADING MAGAZINE OF SELF-DEFENSE

MAY 1971 60 CENTS
46182

BLACK BELT

DOUBLE-BLADED THREAT OF THAI SWORD FIGHTING
HOW TO TAPE WRIST INJURIES

JUDO'S FORGOTTEN PIONEER • TODAY'S LIVING NINJA

ISSUE EIGHTY-NINE | MAY 1971

The 89th issue of *Black Belt* was dated May 1971. It was 66 pages long and featured two *krabi krabong* practitioners on the cover.

Vol. 9, No. 5, 60 cents

▶ After the big San Fernando earthquake in the Los Angles area (magnitude 6.6), Chuck Norris has one *dojo* that's cut off because of road damage and downed phone lines and another that suffered several broken windows. *Black Belt's* offices are undamaged.

▶ Thailand lifts its ban on the Chinese martial arts, allowing kung fu and *tai chi* to emerge from the shadow world of the secret societies in which they were being perpetuated there. Meanwhile, *taekwondo* is the Southeast Asian nation's fastest-growing style.

▶ While taking a potshot at unscrupulous martial arts instructors, former Editor M. Uyehara writes: "There are some dojo operators who thrive on students discontinuing their lessons [after signing a long-term contract]. In fact, some operators simply cannot make a good profit if their students remain in the dojo."

▶ A New Jersey reader questions the validity of the claims made by martial artists who insist they can pulverize other stylists. "Try putting these guys up against the leader of a system such as Fumio Demura, Mas Oyama or Gogen Yamaguchi," he writes. "I bet it would be a different story."

▶ Here's one for the sometimes-we-forget-how-lucky-we-are department: Obsessed with learning *iaido,* Michael Wong of Honolulu writes, "It is surprising that there are no available books in English on the subject."

▶ Ten-year-old Prince Hiro, son of Japanese Crown Prince Akihito and Princess Michiko, takes up *kendo.*

▶ Scam alert: A firm promises men (and women) that they can grow several inches taller if they follow the teachings of a new course. To find out more, it costs 25 cents.

▶ *Black Belt* introduces the Western world to krabi krabong, a rare Thai art of blades, spears and empty hands.

▶ Norihiro Iga-Hakuyusai, a self-proclaimed ninja, wows the Japanese with his demonstrations of martial prowess, but rival *ninjutsu* stylists have branded him a fake.

▶ Chuck Norris guest-stars on the popular TV series *Room 222.* You're probably not old enough to remember that show. ...

▶ In an article profiling American women in the martial arts, upstart *judoka* Jane Orr proclaims: "I don't think American women really care about their health and how they look. Many women are just fat pigs!"

WORLD'S LEADING MAGAZINE OF SELF-DEFENSE

JUNE 1971 60 CENTS
46182

BLACK BELT

OKINAWA'S VERSATILE FIGHTING WEAPONS

JUDO DUMMIES NEVER WIN

POWER WITHOUT STRENGTH

ISSUE NINETY | JUNE 1971

T he 90th issue of *Black Belt* was dated June 1971. It was 66 pages long and featured Tadashi Yamashita on the cover.

Vol. 9, No. 6, 60 cents

▶ A slew of readers write in to defend Mas Oyama, who was reamed by an animal lover who saw the 1970 *Black Belt* Yearbook article in which he discussed his barehanded bouts with bulls.

▶ In a tirade directed at the state of the martial arts, Editor M. Uyehara says, "The old adage that when a *sensei* works for money, the quality of his instruction and skill will eventually deteriorate is possibly becoming a reality, especially in the States."

▶ In a clash of the titans, Fumio Demura faces Kiyoshi Yamazaki for an exhibition match at Orange Coast Junior College in Costa Mesa, California. Their mission is to get karate into the school's physical-education department.

▶ Gosen Yamaguchi, eldest son of *goju-kai* karate founder Gogen "The Cat" Yamaguchi, disappoints his father's followers when he back-burners his karate training because of his new job with Japan Airlines.

▶ Philadelphia prepares its postal carriers to deal with rising numbers of drug addicts who are stealing packages from loading ramps by equipping a squad of 29 men and one woman with firearms and karate training.

▶ The most popular foreign martial art in Thailand is judo. More than 4,000 locals are believed to practice it.

▶ With help from Tadashi Yamashita, *Black Belt* introduces Okinawan weaponry to the Western world: the *tonfa, kusari-gama, kama, sai, nunte, bo* and *nunchaku.* While explaining their uses, he says, "Many people believe self-defense is self-defense and *kata* is kata. This is not true. Every self-defense technique can be found within the kata movements."

▶ The highest-ranked foreign woman in judo is now Margot Sathaye of Great Britain. She's a fourth-degree black belt.

▶ *Sports Illustrated* announces plans to cover the 1971 National Black Belt Karate Championships. ABC may do likewise for its *Wide World of Sports* program.

▶ "There are no secrets in *aikido;* the basic principle, as set forth by Morihei Uyeshiba, is oneness with nature." So says fourth-degree black belt Rod Kobayashi, president of the Aikido Institute of America.

▶ Korean rules—no grabbing or face-punching—handicap American martial artists at the third Foreigners Taekwondo Championships in Seoul, South Korea.

▶ Gene LeBell drops by while the wrestling team is working out at Los Angeles City College. Responding to an invitation to roll, the *gi*-clad LeBell handily defeats three challengers.

WORLD'S LEADING MAGAZINE OF SELF-DEFENSE

JULY 1971
46182   60 CENTS

BLACK BELT

THROUGH KARATE,
HE FOUND
HIMSELF

HOW TO 'SWEEP' YOUR OPPONENT

'THERE ARE NO DEADLY TECHNIQUES IN KARATE'   Gosei Yamaguchi

ISSUE NINETY-ONE | JULY 1971

The 91st issue of *Black Belt* was dated July 1971. It was 66 pages long and featured Bob Dunek (kicking) and Jerry Littlebridge on the cover.

Vol. 9, No. 7, 60 cents

▶ When asked about his dream fight, rising star Bob Dunek says he'd like to face one of his instructors, Mike Stone. "I'd probably get the heck beat out of me," he says, "but you always want to see if your idols live up to your image of them."

▶ Bob Dunek's definition of the complete karate fighter: one with the hands of Stone, the round kick of Bill Wallace, the side kick and back knuckle of Joe Lewis, the heel kick of Skipper Mullins and the reverse punch of Jerry Piddington.

▶ A reader from Illinois implores the martial arts community to put an end to tournaments that are being hailed by the media as "blood baths and race riots."

▶ "It isn't necessary to master all the principles and techniques [of kung fu] to become proficient," says Kah Wah Lee of Malaysia. "You can become a very potent fighter by handling three or four techniques well."

▶ In his criticism of "unbendable arm" demos, Robert H. Martinez opines: "I have seen the same tricks performed by [*aikido* expert Koichi] Tohei, and they are just that—tricks. Mr. Tohei, whose arms are the size of [tree] trunks and who is built like a tank, would clearly have no problem resisting my efforts."

▶ An inventor/*karateka* in Kobe, Japan, has created an electronic vest that uses a light bulb to signal when a solid kick or punch is scored.

▶ Scandal rocks the Nippon Budokan hall in Japan when charges of embezzlement and misappropriation of funds are leveled.

▶ Gosei Yamaguchi, son of *goju* founder Gogen "The Cat" Yamaguchi, describes karate as "a model to live by, involving emotion, violence, mental and physical discipline, coordination and philosophy—all the elements of living."

▶ American air marshals are being trained in judo and the use of firearms. Their counterparts in Israel are learning karate, as well.

▶ *Jujutsu* makes an appearance on the hit TV show *Mission: Impossible*.

▶ Martial artists in Thailand organize a *krabi krabong* tournament, where the hands-down highlight is a dual-sword duel between two girls.

▶ At the All-Karate Championships in New York, Aaron Banks announces that Joe Lewis wants to fight Muhammad Ali. Some members of the crowd believe the challenge is racially motivated.

▶ In South Korea, practitioners of *charyeok* wow audiences with demos in which cars drive over their abdomens. One such school in Seoul reportedly has 900 members—but only 80 active students. Could the other 820 be ... dead?

WORLD'S LEADING MAGAZINE OF SELF-DEFENSE
BLACK BELT
47250
AUG. 1971
60 CENTS
EXCLUSIVE
DON'T BE A VICTIM OF CRIME
Law Enforcement Advisors Tell
What To Do---What Not To Do
plus
FBI Reports Crime Rate
at All-Time High
JEWISH DEFENSE LEAGUE
A Militant Organization
Uses Vigilante Karate.
Is It a Threat to the Art?
PRO WRESTLING:
Is It the Ultimate
in Self-Defense?
GENE LeBELL, Two-Time AAU
Judo Champ and Pro Wrestler,
Reveals Limitations in Martial Arts

ISSUE NINETY-TWO | AUGUST 1971

The 92nd issue of *Black Belt* was dated August 1971. It was 66 pages long and featured a photo of Gene LeBell attempting to throw pro-wrestler Freddie Blassie on the cover.

Vol. 9, No. 8, 60 cents

► Bruce Lee is approached by Hong Kong movie producer Run Run Shaw. "So far, Bruce hasn't committed himself, but if the offer is good enough, he might be tempted," C. Morgan reports.

► The outspoken Gene LeBell, a former professional wrestler and AAU judo champ, unleashes a diatribe against judo. It's titled "Amateurs Teach Amateurs to Be Amateurs."

► A reader from Philadelphia lambastes *Black Belt* over its coverage of a karate tournament: "If true karate ever succeeds in this country, it will be in spite of your efforts to the contrary."

► "Does anyone know the true art of *taekwondo?*" asks an American woman living in Ulsan, South Korea. "Here, it is a combination of karate, boxing and judo."

► A pair of genuine leather focus mitts, called Karate Focusers, sells for $29.95.

► When Jhoon Rhee advocates using a gouge to the eyes and punch to the throat to escape from a front choke, it causes a reader to question the morality of lethality. "It's like shooting a rat with a bazooka," he writes.

► After spending seven years teaching in Los Angeles, renowned karate *sensei* Tak Kubota, 37, proclaims that American students learn more but know less.

► A South Korean pastor stirs up controversy when he begins teaching taekwondo to his congregation. His motivation: The continuing disruption of his church services by rowdy teenagers.

► Members of the Jewish Defense League in the Big Apple take up karate for self-preservation on the city's mean streets. Their weapon of choice is the *nunchaku*—which, by the way, has just been outlawed in the city.

► Syria holds its first national judo championship.

► A medium-size *hakama (aikido* skirt) sells for $8.80. Add 80 cents for large.

► Chuck Norris, Jhoon Rhee, Mike Stone and Mike Anderson meet in St. Louis to brainstorm ways to rejuvenate tournament karate. Their solution: Launch the National Karate League, which will be composed of five-man teams based in major cities around the United States. Fast-forward to 2006, when Norris unveils the World Combat League, an organization made up of martial arts teams based in various cities.

► Two Japanese martial arts masters visit San Diego to school California cops in less-violent methods of crowd control. "They are trained in the art of subduing people without leaving any mark of violence," their translator says.

WORLD'S LEADING MAGAZINE OF SELF-DEFENSE

BLACK BELT

47250
SEPT. 1971
60 CENTS

BRUCE LEE SLAMS CONFORMITY

HOW ZEN COMPLEMENTS THE ART OF KARATE

THE 1971 AAU JUDO CHAMPIONSHIPS

A GUN IN YOUR BACK

"WAKE UP!" BRUCE LEE
Warns Today's Martial Artists,
"You're Being Turned Into Machines!"

What Are Your Options
When An Assailant Demands
"Your Money or Your Life!"?

Issue Ninety-Three | September 1971

The 93rd issue of *Black Belt* was dated September 1971. It was 66 pages long and featured a photo of a mustachioed Bruce Lee on the cover.

Vol. 9, No. 9, 60 cents

▶ Bruce Lee offers up perhaps his most famous treatise: "Liberate Yourself From Classical Karate." Among its best-known gems are his references to partial truth versus whole truth, *jeet kune do* being merely a name, having no form and the finger pointing at the moon.

▶ When the editor of *Black Belt* questions a cool cat about his refusal to accept the custom of bowing in the *dojo,* he replies: "Very few of us are interested in *bushido* philosophy. We are in the United States, man, not in old Japan. What counts here is winning and making some dough."

▶ *Shotokan* spreads to Hong Kong. A new branch of the Japan Karate Association is organized in the British colony with a membership of 75.

▶ California native Cal Martin is working his way up through the sumo ranks in Japan. Two years ago, he weighed 205 pounds. Now, he's 275. The secret of his success: pizza, spaghetti and Hawaiian Punch.

▶ A 7-year-old *karateka* takes America by storm, with stints on *The Mike Douglas Show, The Today Show, What's My Line?, To Tell the Truth* and the Paul Harvey radio show. Next up for the kid and her family: An appearance with her 15-month-old brother, who will attempt to break a board.

▶ The New York Radical Feminists take to karate. "Since you are living in a jungle and no one may help you, be self-reliant," Mary Ann Manhart says. "Everyone has a tiger inside of her."

▶ Parisians are going nuts over the *yamasuki,* a new Japanese disco dance that incorporates a number of karate moves, as well as "the karateka's grunts, hisses and shouts."

▶ Douglas Nelson takes top honors at the 1971 Senior AAU Judo Nationals in St. Louis. Among the other winners are Hayward Nishioka, Pat Burris and Allen Coage.

▶ American International Pictures releases *Taboos of the World,* which describes dojo sparring as the "discipline of death" and promises it will be "revealed for the first time."

▶ The Dominican Republic hosts a new concept in competition: a *taekwondo*-versus-*kenpo* tournament. The results speak volumes, with students of the Jhoon Rhee Institute snagging 10 out of 12 first-place trophies.

▶ According to a recent survey, 6 percent of *Black Belt's* readership is female.

▶ Riled up after reading *Black Belt's* report on the bull-busting Mas Oyama, an animal lover fires back: "It's certainly not humane to twist and break their necks after having punched them between their blindfolded eyes. Obviously, Oyama has studied the physical weaknesses of bulls. The bull is deprived of that opportunity."

▶ A karate-practicing Zen monk from Japan offers his opinion on the state of the martial arts in the United States: "The emphasis Americans seem to place on fighting and breaking boards and comparing styles is distressing." Thank you very much, Bodhidharma!

THE 1971 YEARBOOK, FEATURING THE WORLD'S TOP RANKED COMPETITORS

BLACK BELT

48243
YEARBOOK '71
$1.00

THE HALL OF FAME: SIX OUTSTANDING MARTIAL ARTISTS OF 1971 HONORED

TIGER vs. CRANE
Gung-Fu's Fury of Fang and Claw

FUNAKOSHI: WHAT KIND OF MAN WAS THE FOUNDER OF MODERN KARATE?

ISSUE NINETY-FOUR | OCTOBER 1971

The 94th issue of *Black Belt* was dated October 1971. Being the Yearbook special, it was 98 pages long. Buck Sam Kong (right) was on the cover.

Vol. 9, No. 10, $1

► The 1971 *Black Belt* Hall of Fame inductees are announced: S. Henry Cho is Man of the Year, Robert Yarnall receives the Karate Sensei Award, George Harris gets the Judo Sensei Award, Maki Miyahara is presented with the Kendo Sensei Award, Paul Maruyama nets the Judo Player Award and Mike Stone wins the Karate Player Award.

► S. Henry Cho demonstrates his kicking skills on *The Tonight Show Starring Johnny Carson.* He even coaxes Carson to bust a board barefooted.

► *Hung gar* legend Buck Sam Kong describes his kung fu training in Hong Kong: "A stick of incense, timed to burn for 45 minutes, was placed in front of the student. He was expected to maintain [the horse] stance until the incense burned out."

► *Black Belt* founder M. Uyehara weighs in on the faltering economy and its effect on the martial arts: "Across the country, karate's front-office men have tried every scheme imaginable to attract the audiences of five years ago but have met with limited success."

► A ranking of the top 10 karate practitioners in the United States includes more than a few familiar names: (in order) Bill Wallace, Joe Hayes , Ron Marchini, Fred Wren, Mitchell Bobrow, Pat Worley, Byong Yu, Bill Watson, Louis Delgado and Joe Corley.

► In a profile of *shotokan* founder Gichin Funakoshi, we're reminded of the master's controversial words: "There are no offensive techniques in karate."

► *Black Belt* presents the results of its 1970 survey of the martial arts: Participation in the striking arts drops to approximately 120,000 from 123,000 in 1969. The breakdown is 41,000 in the Japanese arts, 56,000 in the Korean arts, 14,000 in the Okinawan arts and 8,500 in miscellaneous arts (*kempo,* kung fu and so on).

► As far as the *dojo* go, 43 percent are Japanese, 27 percent are Korean, 17 percent are Okinawan and 13 percent are devoted to those miscellaneous arts.

► The second Asian Taekwondo Tournament takes place in Malaysia. Gen. Choi Hong-hi, founder of the Korean art, is the guest of honor.

► Kickboxing makes its debut in the Big Apple at Aaron Banks' United Nations Open Karate Championship. In the main event, Joe Lewis defeats Ron Barkoot with a first-round knockout.

► A reader from Tokyo prods *Black Belt* to stop using the term "black belt" to refer to people who've attained the rank of ... black belt. Among his reasons is that "it takes less space to print *shodan.*"

WORLD'S LEADING MAGAZINE OF SELF-DEFENSE

BLACK BELT

47250
NOV. 1971
60 CENTS

"COMPETITION KARATE IS NO GAME!"

Two Karate-Fighting Brothers Reveal How They Command Respect From Opponents

OTSUKA—The Living Legend Who Put Combat In Karate.

DANGER LURKS In A Deserted Garage. How Can You Protect Yourself?

ISSUE NINETY-FIVE | NOVEMBER 1971

The 95th issue of *Black Belt* was dated November 1971. It was 66 pages long and featured brothers Bob and Ralph Alegria on the cover.

Vol. 9, No. 11, 60 cents

► Plans are announced for Bruce Lee to guest-star in *Longstreet,* a series about a blind insurance investigator. Lee will teach self-defense to star James Franciscus in an episode titled "The Way of the Intercepting Fist."

► The Koreans are coming! The Koreans are coming! Rumor has it that South Korea's Yudo College is preparing to send 160 judo instructors to the United States to take over collegiate judo. Meanwhile, the number of people teaching the Korean stand-up arts in the States has quadrupled in the past five years.

► The most recent Asia Judo Championships reveals the real powerhouses of grappling: 1. Japan, 2. South Korea, 3. Taiwan, 4. Philippines and 5. Indonesia.

► Karate is making inroads in Sweden. The country boasts 30 *dojo* with a combined membership of more than 1,000.

► *Hawaii Five-O* actor Roy Sukimoto is threatened with disqualification from the AAU Senior Judo Nationals because his hair is long enough to touch his collar.

► "Fighting side by side on a team with other top fighters is stimulating, but a man should fight alone until he realizes who he is," says Bob Alegria, a California-based karate champ and dojo operator.

► In a Tokyo museum, a 23-year-old student smashes a display case, retrieves two 14th-century samurai swords and kills himself.

► *Black Belt* introduces *glimae,* a rare form of Icelandic wrestling, to the martial arts world.

► Japanese karate master Hironori Otsuka, 79, unveils *wado-kai,* a new form of fighting that mixes *kempo, jujutsu* and karate.

► Ray Edler is the only Caucasian kickboxer competing in Japan.

► *Judoka* Yukio Maeda, 29, collapses and dies during a tournament at the Kodokan in Tokyo. The cause of death is listed as myocardial infarction.

► Ken Knudsen releases a home-study course called *Circle System of Self-Defense.* It includes six cassette tapes, a 58-page booklet and a 12-inch-by-12-inch striking block. The cost is $49.95.

► In "How to Disarm a Gunman," renowned author and trainer Massad F. Ayoob offers sage advice for self-defense: "An armed assailant can be considered neutralized only if he is rendered completely unconscious or his gun hand is immobilized."

WORLD'S LEADING MAGAZINE OF SELF-DEFENSE

BLACK BELT

47250
DEC. 1971
60 CENTS

CAN YOU MAKE BIG MONEY FROM KARATE TOURNAMENTS?

The Rags to Riches Story of Aaron Banks, Nation's Most Controversial Matchmaker.

JUJITSU: WORLD WAR 1 STYLE
DON'T LAUGH! IT'S FOR REAL.

ATTACK IN A PUBLIC WASHROOM--
DON'T LET IT HAPPEN TO YOU!

ACUPUNCTURE, THE ANCIENT CHINESE
ART OF NEEDLE THERAPY. CAN IT REALLY
IMPROVE THE POWER OF THE KI?

ISSUE NINETY-SIX | DECEMBER 1971

The 96th issue of *Black Belt* was dated December 1971. It was 66 pages long and featured a painting of Aaron Banks on the cover.

Vol. 9, No. 12, 60 cents

▶ MMA alert! A new strain of kickboxing that's becoming popular in Japan is a combination of karate, boxing, judo, wrestling and head butts. Some 1,200 martial artists currently compete in it.

▶ Dutch judo legend Anton Geesink enrages America when he declares that U.S. judo is still "in the Stone Age." The culprit isn't laziness, he says. It's the teaching method.

▶ In a separate story, Korean *judoka* Kyung Sun Shin unknowingly chimes in on the problem: "Very strange ... in Korea, students chase instructor; in U.S., instructor chases students."

▶ Bruce Lee leaves for a three-month stint in Hong Kong and Thailand, where he'll film two kung fu flicks. Meanwhile, ABC execs are so thrilled with Lee's recent appearance on *Longstreet* that they ask him to do three more episodes.

▶ A 5-foot-1-inch, 95-pound female reader writes to express her concerns about using her karate skills on the street: "If [a woman is] not a skilled fighter, her only advantage against vastly superior strength lies in surprise."

▶ In the five years since Aikikai *aikido* instructor Hiroshi Tada set up shop in Rome, he's promoted 24 black belts. They may be the only ones in Italy.

▶ For the first time, Malaysia unveils the ancient art of *silat seni gayong*.

▶ A female judoka from Minnesota is appalled that the Australian judo community has apparently decided to remove mat work and sacrifices from women's competition. "Real *shiai* requires more than just throwing techniques," she says.

▶ When asked about his predictions for the future of the martial arts in America, promoter Aaron Banks says, "I see the Koreans taking over karate because they are so well organized, and I see kickboxing supplanting karate in the public's favor."

▶ TV advertising is the ticket to success. Jhoon Rhee and Chuck Norris are the first to try it for their schools, and Aaron Banks is considering using it to spread the word about his next tournament.

▶ *Billy Jack* is released in theaters, showcasing the talents of *hapkido* expert Bong Soo Han and his student, star Tom Laughlin.

▶ For $15.50, visitors to Tokyo can take a five-hour tour of various sumo-related facilities. Among the most fascinating sights is a museum exhibit of *mawashi,* or sumo thongs.

WORLD'S LEADING MAGAZINE OF SELF-DEFENSE

BLACK BELT

47250
JAN. 1972
60 CENTS

HOW TO SWEEP YOUR OPPONENT
AAU CHAMP JUDOKA AND KARATEKA NISHIOKA SHOWS HOW TO FLATTEN A FOE!

SHOULD KARATE NOT BE TAUGHT TO KIDS?
Japanese Sensei Believes Karate Breeds
Overconfidence In Youngsters.

KARATE TRAINING CANNOT ELIMINATE AGGRESSION!
A Psychologist—Karate
Sensei Explains Why Real
Aggressions Can Never Be
Overcome.

KILL WITHOUT QUESTION!
The Hired Killer Performed His Duties
Mercilessly... Until He Made One Mistake.

1971 WORLD JUDO CHAMPIONSHIPS RESULTS!

ISSUE NINETY-SEVEN | JANUARY 1972

The 97th issue of *Black Belt* was dated January 1972. It was 66 pages long and featured a photo of *judoka* Hayward Nishioka on the cover.

Vol. 10, No. 1, 60 cents

▶ Regarding Bruce Lee's recent appearance on an episode of *Longstreet* titled "The Way of the Intercepting Fist," Carl G. Henderson writes: "I feel a great deal of relief knowing that people have seen a true dimension of the martial arts. For many years, I have secluded the fact that I studied the arts because I had tired of the ignorant attitudes and positions taken by co-workers and friends."

▶ Noriyasu Kudo—a Springfield, Massachusetts-based karate instructor who's studied sumo, judo, *kendo* and boxing—claims that American martial artists learn too many techniques too soon and spend too much time doing *kata*.

▶ A gaggle of readers write in response to Bruce Lee's now-famous "Liberate Yourself From Classical Karate." One of the best letters comes from a man from the the Bronx, New York: "Liberate ourselves from karate? No, my friend, with due respect, that particular chance could never come into my life. Karate is my life, and it's my world."

▶ The number of readers who voice their opinions about Gene LeBell's controversial "Amateurs Teach Amateurs to Be Amateurs," in which he lauds wrestling over the martial arts, is only slightly lower. To one of the most fiery, a *jujutsu* stylist, LeBell replies, "I approve of all arts of physical combat. ... Jujutsu, as taught by an all-encompassing teacher, is an outstanding form of self-defense. ... I'm very set in my opinion that any art of self-defense that does not have free sparring cannot reach the zenith."

▶ The state of the art in training weapons: A featureless slab of foam rubber shaped like a .45 and dipped in vinyl. Your cost: $1.95.

▶ Lee Alexander, the mayor of Syracuse, New York, announces the creation of Karate Day in his city, then busts a board with his fist.

▶ The President's Council on Physical Fitness recognizes judo as a competitive sport but complains that the various factions are weakening the art in the United States.

▶ Ken Knudsen begins giving free karate lessons to public-school teachers in Chicago after 269 educators are assaulted in a two-month period. In his free time, he just completed *Circle System of Self-Defense*, a home-study course that includes six cassette tapes, a 58-page booklet and a striking block—all for $49.95.

▶ Hayward Nishioka advises self-defense-oriented *karateka* to supplement their skills with judo's offensive and defensive methods: "A karate fighter who finds himself flat on his back as the result of a cleanly executed foot sweep is at a distinct disadvantage in trying to defend himself."

▶ It's been revealed: A recent newspaper article titled "Karate Expert Commits Suicide by Kicking Himself to Death" is a hoax.

▶ If judo founder Jigoro Kano could feel the power of today's judoka, he "would turn over in his grave," says 207-pound, third-degree *sensei* Wally Barber.

▶ Ready for a little R&R? Pick up a new board game called Black Belt Master Karate Expert. Designed by a *kenpo* stylist, it forces participants who receive a penalty card to do sit-ups and push-ups, jog in place or stand on one leg. Lose a "sparring match" and you'll have to start over at the beginning. It's yours for only $5.

WORLD'S LEADING MAGAZINE OF SELF-DEFENSE

BLACK BELT

47250
FEB. 1972
60 CENTS

KICK-BOXING: HEADED FOR SAME CHAOS AS KARATE?
U.S. PROMOTERS FIGHT FOR CONTROL OF THAILAND'S ANCIENT MARTIAL ART

A BAD BOY WHO WOULDN'T AMOUNT TO ANYTHING
BECAME JUDO'S GREATEST TACTICIAN AND THE LAST OF ITS HONORED GODS

NUNCHAKU
FOR TRAINING, NOT DESTROYING!
It can improve your karate....
IF PROPERLY USED!

'EVERYONE HAS FORGOTTEN WHAT KARATE REALLY IS,'
SAYS AN UNCONVENTIONAL SENSEI WHOSE STUDENTS INCLUDE
EX-HELL'S ANGELS, PRO BOXERS AND POLIO VICTIMS